THE PATH TO WAR

U.S. MARINE CORPS OPERATIONS IN SOUTHEAST ASIA

1961 TO 1965

COLONEL GEORGE R. HOFMANN JR., U.S. MARINE CORPS (RETIRED)

MARINES IN THE VIETNAM WAR COMMEMORATIVE SERIES

This pamphlet history, one in a series devoted to U.S. Marines in the Vietnam War, is published for the education and training of Marines by the History Division, Marine Corps University, Quantico, Virginia, as part of the U.S. Department of Defense observance of the fiftieth anniversary of that war. Editorial costs have been defrayed in part by contributions from members of the Marine Corps Heritage Foundation.

Marines in the Vietnam War Commemorative Series

Director of Marine Corps History
Dr. Charles P. Neimeyer

Chief Historian of the Marine Corps
Charles D. Melson

Senior Editor
Angela J. Anderson

Vietnam War Commemorative Series Editor
Shawn H. Vreeland

Visual Information Specialist
Robert A. Kocher

2014

This narrative chronicles the activities of the U.S. Marine Corps in Southeast Asia from January 1961 to March 1965. The period witnesses increasing Marine Corps involvement in the region as our nation's leaders responded to Communist aggression and sought to protect the United States' national interests. Individual Marines saw duty as early as 1954 when a Marine lieutenant colonel was assigned to the U.S. Military Assistance Advisory Group (MAAG) in Saigon, South Vietnam. The first involvement of a Marine Corps operational unit came in March 1961 with the deployment to Udorn, Thailand, of approximately 300 Marines from Marine Air Base Squadron 16 (MABS-16). The squadron's mission was to provide aircraft maintenance and flight-line support operations for Air America, a U.S. company flying missions in support of the pro-Western forces in Laos. MABS-16 remained in northeast Thailand for seven months, not returning to its home base at Futema, Okinawa, until Air America had become self-supporting in October 1961.

The situation in Laos continued to deteriorate, and in early 1962 Communist aggression was threatening to spill over into neighboring Thailand. President John F. Kennedy's administration, determined to protect this vitally important Asian ally and Southeast Asia Treaty Organization (SEATO) member, ordered the 3d Marine Expeditionary Brigade (3d MEB) to deploy to Thailand in May 1962 as a "show of force" and as a demonstration of American resolve to halt the spread of Communism in Southeast Asia. As the situation in Laos stabilized, the 3d MEB, which in fact was reduced in size and actually deployed as a Marine expeditionary unit, began an incremental withdrawal with all Marines departing Thailand by the end of July 1962.

Earlier, individual Marines had been posted to South Vietnam, where they served in a variety of roles. Prior to the signing of the 1954 Geneva Agreement that partitioned Vietnam at the 17th parallel, a Marine guard detachment had been assigned to provide embassy security. In addition, several Marines were assigned to the MAAG staff and, when it was established, to the U.S. Military Assistance Command, Vietnam (USMACV).

When the South Vietnamese Marine Corps (VNMC) was established on 13 October 1954, U.S. Marine advisors—both officers and enlisted men—were assigned to provide training, operational, and logistic support. As the VNMC expanded over time, the number of U.S. Marine advisors assigned also grew. In 1961, the commanding general of Fleet Marine Force, Pacific (FMFPac), initiated an On-the-Job Training (OJT) Program that assigned 3d Marine Division (3d MarDiv) and 1st Marine Aircraft Wing (1st MAW) junior officers and staff noncommissioned officers to Republic of Vietnam (RVN) military units for 30 days to observe combat operations. In response to increasing Viet Cong[*] and North Vietnamese Army (NVA) operations in South Vietnam and to providing the Army of the Republic of Vietnam

---

[*] A derogatory term coined by Ngo Dinh Diem's government that is short for Viet Nam Cong San and usually translated as "Vietnamese Communist." Not all Viet Cong were Communists, however; some just wanted foreigners to withdraw from Vietnam.

(ARVN) with much-needed tactical mobility, a Marine medium helicopter squadron with supporting elements was ordered to South Vietnam and arrived on 15 April 1962. In the closing months of 1964, the Marine Corps began assigning officers and enlisted Marines as advisors to the ARVN divisions operating in South Vietnam's I Corps Tactical Zone (I Corps).

The OJT Program, the advisors to the VNMC and ARVN units, and the Marine medium helicopter squadron represented the most visible Marine Corps contributions to the defense of South Vietnam until the major buildup of forces began in March 1965. However, increasing numbers of Marines were also assigned to the MAAG and USMACV staffs as the U.S. commitment to assist South Vietnam grew in the early 1960s. In addition, during the period before major forces were committed to Vietnam, several small Marine Corps organizations—often communications units—deployed to South Vietnam for short periods. By early 1965, the number of Marines in South Vietnam exceeded 800.

The Early Years

Following the end of World War II, the French returned to reassert their control over all of colonial Indochina. Their return was not widely accepted; rather, it was met with an organized and determined resistance. Beginning in the 1920s, but particularly during World War II, Ho Chi Minh—a fierce nationalist but also a dedicated Communist—had established a political party and then transformed it into a sizeable and well-organized guerrilla force—the Viet Nam Doc Lap Dong Minh Hoi (League for the Independence of Vietnam), known simply as the Viet Minh. After the war, he employed this force to frustrate French efforts to reestablish their authority. Ho's first objective was the full independence that he and his followers believed would come with the end of the war. When independence was not forthcoming and the French return proved inevitable, Ho made accommodations with them. At the same time, however, he sabotaged their efforts to regain control with the long-term goal of permanently ejecting them from all of Indochina.

The French attempted to reassert their control over Indochina by granting the colony's component regions autonomy within the French Union as associated states. In 1949, Laos

and Cambodia both concluded agreements with France, making them associated states within the union and granting them limited self-government. That same year, the French also formally created the State of Vietnam in order to create an effective bulwark against the Communist Viet Minh forces. Led by Chief of State Bao Dai (who, in 1945, had abdicated his role as emperor of Vietnam at Ho Chi Minh's insistence), the state, like Laos and Cambodia, remained within the French Union.

The French achieved some early successes, reasserting their control in the major cities and over the major transportation systems. Despite these gains, their rule was challenged by Ho Chi Minh's guerrilla forces that, as a result of their organizing and military activities prior to and during World War II, were firmly entrenched in the countryside surrounding the major population centers. In a classic insurgent struggle, where the stronger power will often lose to the initially weaker force, the road-bound and logistics-dependent French steadily lost ground to the more agile, lighter equipped Viet Minh. Between 1946 and early 1954, the Viet Minh grew steadily stronger and more capable as they transitioned through the three phases of Mao Tse-tung's well-known guerrilla strategy. On 7 May 1954, after a painful and debilitating set-piece battle in a valley on the Vietnam-Laos border known as Dien Bien Phu, the French force of slightly more than 10,000 men was forced to surrender to the larger and stronger Viet Minh that, by this time, was organized and fighting in division strength.

Although the force defending Dien Bien Phu represented only about 5 percent of the French force then deployed in Indochina, the psychological effect of the defeat turned the war-weary French public, media, and government against any continuation of the war in Indochina. At a conference held in Geneva—convened only immediately before the French capitulation at Dien Bien Phu—diplomats from both democratic and Communist nations that had gathered to consider a peace agreement for Korea also sought to resolve the Indochina conflict. On 20 July 1954, the Geneva Agreement granted Vietnam, Laos, and Cambodia complete independence. Also agreed upon was a temporary partition of Vietnam along the Ben Hai River (roughly at the 17th parallel) with the stated purpose of facilitating the disengagement of opposing forces. Reunification would come, the agreement required, with democratic elections to be held in both the north and the south in mid-1956.

In the north, Ho Chi Minh quickly established the Democratic Republic of Vietnam (DRV), with its capital in Hanoi. In the south—which retained the State of Vietnam as its name—political power passed to the French-supported former emperor, Bao Dai; however, real power resided in the pro-Western, anti-Communist, and Catholic premier, Ngo Dinh Diem.

The months immediately following the Geneva Agreement found Ngo Dinh Diem consolidating power and establishing a working government in the south, with its capital in Saigon. Opposition came from three sources: the former emperor Bao Dai (who was residing in France); local, sect-based rival armies in the provinces surrounding Saigon; and a crime syndicate. The key to success was control of the poorly organized Vietnamese National Army, which had been established by the French to support their operations against the Viet Minh. In a period stretching over a year, Diem successfully managed to marginalize his opposition, and on 26 October 1955, after approval by a national referendum, he proclaimed the formation of the RVN, with himself as its president.

In the north, with government and military structures already in place, Ho Chi Minh continued to organize. He reconstituted his 240,000 battle-tested Viet Minh force, forming the People's Army of Vietnam. Both the Soviet Union and Communist China—in violation of the Geneva Agreement—provided weapons and equipment to Ho's forces.

Provisions of the Geneva Agreement called for the regrouping of opposing military forces to their respective sides of the partition line within 300 days of the agreement's signing. It also allowed civilians on either side of the partition line to emigrate to the other side in accordance with their

Mao Tse-tung's Three-Phase Model for Protracted War

In their efforts to overthrow the legitimate government and take control of South Vietnam, the leadership of the DRV adhered closely to Mao Tse-tung's three-phase model. It comprises the following parts that continue and build upon the preceding phases:

- Phase I involves "guerrilla warfare" in which small bands of insurgents, lacking permanent bases and popular support, employ hit-and-run tactics against small units of the legitimate government's armed forces.

- Phase II shifts the strategy to "mobile warfare" in which organized insurgent military units of company, battalion, and regiment size conduct selected and limited engagements against the forces of the legitimately constituted government. During this phase, increasing amounts of the population and territory come under the insurgents' control, and their political and military strength grows.

- Phase III shifts efforts into "general offensive" mode in which the population rallies to the insurgents' cause, and insurgent military units of up to division size engage the legitimate government's forces and defeat them.

The Western Pacific

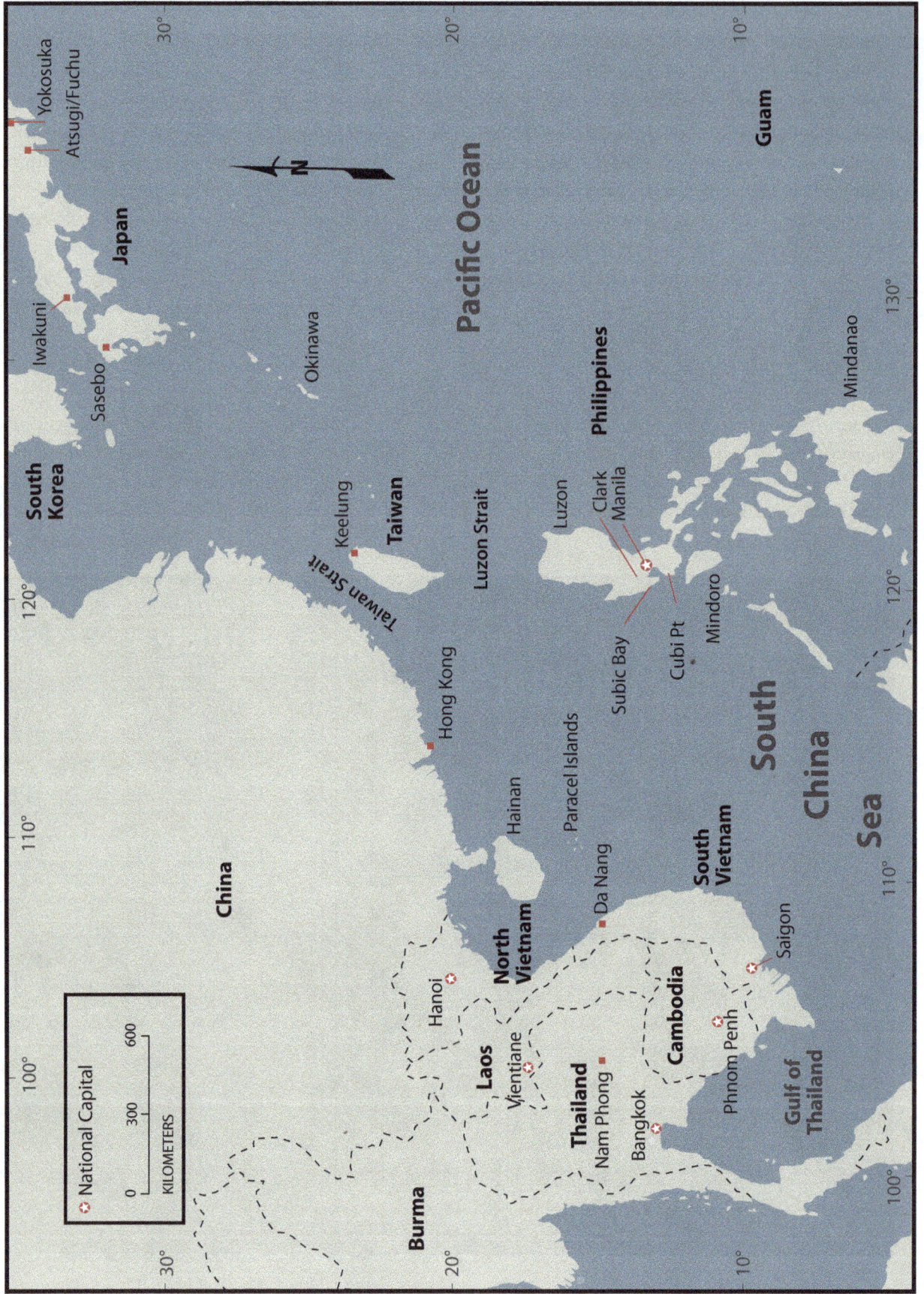

China

Burma

Laos

Thailand

North Vietnam

South Vietnam

Cambodia

Hanoi

Vientiane

Nam Phong

Bangkok

Phnom Penh

Saigon

Da Nang

Gulf of Thailand

Hainan

Paracel Islands

Hong Kong

Taiwan Strait

Keelung

Taiwan

Luzon Strait

Luzon

Clark
Manila

Subic Bay

Cubi Pt

Mindoro

Philippines

Mindanao

South Korea

Japan

Yokosuka

Atsugi/Fuchu

Iwakuni

Sasebo

Okinawa

Pacific Ocean

Guam

South China Sea

National Capital

0   300   600

KILOMETERS

N

30°

20°

10°

130°

120°

110°

100°

120°

110°

100°

30°

20°

10°

political convictions. The months following the July agreement saw nearly a million people depart the north to live in the south. Many Viet Minh soldiers, whose homes and families were in the south, were sent to the north for education and training before being introduced back into their home villages in the south. Further, the Viet Minh intentionally left between 5,000 and 10,000 men in the south to form an initial cadre of forces dedicated to the overthrow of the Diem regime, or any other follow-on government in the south.

Early U.S. Involvement

The United States' involvement in Indochina predates the 1954 departure of the French. America's containment strategy, developed to stop the spread of Communism in the years following World War II and initially focused on the expansionist Soviet Union, was extended to China after Mao Tse-tung's Communist forces drove Chiang Kai-shek's nationalist army off the mainland in 1949. With North Korea's invasion of South Korea in summer 1950, and a deteriorating situation in Indochina, Harry S. Truman's administration came to fear that the entire Asian mainland was in danger of falling under Communist domination. Accordingly, President Truman extended America's containment policy to Indochina.

The U.S. Congress supported this action and quickly appropriated $4 billion that was added to military assistance funds. Much of this funding flowed to the French to support their operations in Indochina. Further, in mid-1950, Truman ordered the establishment of a MAAG to provide logistical support to the French Expeditionary Corps. Establishing this MAAG created the infrastructure through which material support was provided to the French. By May 1954, when the French capitulated to the Viet Minh at Dien Bien Phu, the United States was funding more than 40 percent of the French effort in Indochina.

Vietnamese Marine Corps and U.S. Marine Advisors: 1954–62

After the Geneva Agreement was signed in July 1954, the United States shifted the focus of its military assistance program in South Vietnam from the French to the newly formed government of Ngo Dinh Diem. Under the command of Army Lieutenant General John M. O'Daniel, who had been assigned to command the MAAG in spring 1954, and the 342 men assigned to his command, the group began the herculean task of building the South Vietnamese armed forces. Delays were encountered while agreements were negotiated between American, South Vietnamese, and French officials. During this initial period, a considerable amount of U.S. assistance continued to flow to French units that were supporting South Vietnamese military organizations. By mid-January 1955, however, arrangements had largely been completed to refocus all training, equipping, and advising functions from the French to the Vietnamese military. It was during this period of transition from French to U.S. control that the first Marine was assigned to the MAAG in Saigon.

By any standard of measure, Lieutenant Colonel Victor J. Croizat had already enjoyed an exceptional and successful career as a Marine. His service, however, was far from over. On 30 June 1954, the assistant chief of staff, G-1, at FMFPac headquarters announced that Croizat would fill the new billet authorized by the Commandant of the Marine Corps (CMC) at the MAAG in Saigon. Upon his arrival on 2 August—which predated the establishment of the VNMC by three months—General O'Daniel assigned Colonel Croizat to serve on the South Vietnamese–created General Commission for Refugees. After a short period overseeing the selection and development of refugee reception and resettlement areas in the south, Croizat traveled to Haiphong—the site of North Vietnam's principal harbor—where he headed the MAAG detachment and coordinated the U.S.-assisted refugee evacuations with those of the French and the Vietnamese. This humanitarian effort, which eventually evacuated 807,000 people; 469,000 tons of equipment and supplies; and 23,000 vehicles, would not be completed until May 1955. Colonel Croizat, however, returned to Saigon in February.

On 13 October 1954 (but with an effective date of 1 October 1954), President Diem established the VNMC by presidential decree. Organized as a component of the Vietnamese naval forces, its initial authorized strength was approximately 2,400 officers and men. Many of the VNMC's initial recruits were men who had recently been evacuated from North Vietnam. They were organized into a landing battalion, six riverboat companies, five combat light-support companies, and a small training flotilla. A former ARVN officer, Major

Colonel Victor J. Croizat

Defense Department (Marine Corps) A104057

Few Marines have enjoyed a more varied and exciting career than Colonel Victor J. Croizat. Born in Tripoli, Libya, on 27 February 1919, he spent his early childhood in Italy and France before his family moved to New York City. After high school he attended Syracuse University where he earned a degree in forestry. Following graduation, he was commissioned a Marine second lieutenant on 8 July 1940.

Croizat served in several of the Corps' toughest World War II campaigns. He went ashore on Guadalcanal on 7 August 1942 as the commanding officer of Company A, 1st Amphibian Tractor Battalion. Later in that engagement, he commanded the machine gun company in the 3d Battalion, 5th Marines. In December 1943, he formed the 10th Amphibian Tractor Battalion, 4th Marine Division, which he then commanded in the assault landings on Kwajalein, Saipan, Tinian, and Iwo Jima. During his World War II combat tours, he earned the Bronze Star Medal with Combat "V" and a Letter of Commendation.

Following postwar overseas and stateside tours, Croizat attended the École Supérieure de Guerre in Paris, France, from September 1949 to November 1950. After graduation, he was ordered to Quantico, Virginia, where he served for three and a half years as a tactics instructor at Senior School (now Command and Staff College). As the Geneva Agreement brought the French colonial period in Southeast Asia to a close, Croizat, in July 1954, received orders to the MAAG in Saigon.

The next month, Croizat was in Haiphong, North Vietnam, where, as the MAAG representative, he supervised the evacuation to South Vietnam of more than a half-million refugees, including their personal possessions and equipment. Returning to South Vietnam in January 1955, Croizat was assigned to the MAAG's Navy Section where he served as the first senior Marine advisor to the newly established VNMC. In this capacity, he influenced significantly the initial organization and training of the Vietnamese marines. He also assisted in the reorganization of the Vietnamese Navy. Upon completion of his tour in August 1956, he was ordered to Washington, DC.

There, Croizat served for three years as the head of the Strategic Plans Section, G-3 Division, at Marine Corps Headquarters. Temporary assignments during this period sent him to Algeria to observe helicopter operations, Haiti to negotiate terms for establishing a Marine Corps mission, and French West Africa and French Equatorial Africa in support of the J-3 Section of the Joint Chiefs of Staff initiatives. During the 1959–60 academic year, Croizat attended the National War College.

In August 1960 he was ordered to the Far East and assumed duties as the chief of staff, Task Force 79, Fleet Marine Force, Seventh Fleet. Less than a year passed before, in May 1961, he was ordered to Bangkok, Thailand. There he served as the U.S. military advisors' representative at SEATO headquarters. Following this assignment, Croizat returned to the United States where, in 1964, he assumed command of the 5th Marines. Two years later, after more than 26 years of service, Colonel Croizat retired from the Marine Corps.

Le Quang Trong, was assigned as the senior marine* officer. As no formal geographic headquarters had been established and no command structure had been included in the table of organization (T/O), Major Trong's ability to control his new command was immediately and severely challenged. Further, his units were spread from Hue in the north to the Mekong River Delta in the south, rendering effective control of his new command difficult at best.

Many French officers were still serving in command positions in the Vietnamese naval forces, making French influence very evident in early VNMC decisions. The landing battalion, which was located at Nha Trang, was actually commanded by a French Army captain. Soon after its establishment, the VNMC was instructed to reduce its strength to 1,137 officers and men, the result of a U.S.-Vietnamese force-level agreement that limited naval forces to a ceiling of 3,000.

When he returned to Saigon in February 1955, Croizat was assigned to the MAAG's Naval Section and designated the senior U.S. advisor to the VNMC. Two additional Marine advisors—Captain James T. Breckinridge and Technical Sergeant Jackson E. Tracy—joined him that summer. Colonel Croizat ordered Captain Breckinridge to Nha Trang to serve as advisor to the lst Landing Battalion. Upon Breckinridge's arrival, the French Army captain was relieved. Initially, Technical Sergeant Tracy remained in Saigon; however, he was later transferred to Nha Trang, where he served as a small unit tactics instructor for the VNMC. The following year, his position was converted to an officer billet.

In 1955, the VNMC's 1st Landing Battalion was called into action. Its opponents were not Communist forces, but the armies and guerrilla forces of the Hoa Hao and Cao Dai sects and the Binh Xuyen, an underworld organization. As noted previously, these organizations posed a genuine threat to the government of Ngo Dinh Diem. In addition to the

Vietnamese marines' landing battalion, Diem committed some 30 additional ARVN battalions to their eradication. In August, the lst Landing Battalion fought a decisive battle against remaining members of the Hoa Hao sect in Kien Giang Province, about 120 miles south of Saigon. During this action, the landing battalion destroyed the sect's headquarters. Later in 1955, the 1st Landing Battalion, augmented by several riverboat companies, eliminated one of the last pockets of Binh Xuyen strength in the Rung Sat swamps, also south of the capital. By year's end, organized resistance to Deim's government had been reduced to an insignificant level, and the Vietnamese marines had firmly established their value. When the 1st Landing Battalion returned to garrison on 7 February 1956, it had been in the field for over seven months.

In summer 1955, the United States approved force-level increases for the Republic of Vietnam Armed Forces. The overall force level was raised from 100,000 to 150,000 and the naval force level was increased to 4,000. Under this and subsequent force-level increases, the VNMC would continue to grow, as would the number of U.S. Marine advisors. While the 1st Landing Battalion was in the field, Colonel Croizat had conducted a review of the entire VNMC structure. The existence of so many dissimilar units on one level led him to recommend to Major Phan Van Lieu, who on 18 January 1956 had relieved Major Trong and assumed command of the VNMC, that the entire organization be restructured. Assisted by his U.S. Marine advisors as well as his own staff, Major Lieu developed a new structure for the VNMC, which was approved by the Vietnamese Joint General Staff. The most important feature of this restructuring was the addition of a second landing battalion, which was accomplished without increasing the VNMC's then-authorized ceiling of 1,837. Also included in the restructuring were a small headquarters section and a 4.2-inch mortar company. The reconstruction plans also contained verbiage proposing a future expansion of the VNMC to regimental size. In spite of this proposal, the Vietnamese marines remained a two-battalion regiment for about the next three years.

---

*For clarity, the term "marine" will be lowercased when referring to South Vietnamese marines except when used with formal unit names, such as the Vietnamese Marine Brigade, and uppercased when referring to U.S. Marines and the U.S. Marine Corps.

```
                    ┌─────────────────────┐
                    │   MARINE INFANTRY   │
                    │    HEADQUARTERS     │
                    └─────────────────────┘
          ┌───────────────────┼───────────────────┐
┌─────────────────────┐ ┌─────────────────────┐ ┌─────────────────────┐
│   HEADQUARTERS AND  │ │  LANDING BATTALIONS │ │      4.2-INCH       │
│   SERVICE COMPANY   │ │         (2)         │ │   MORTAR COMPANY    │
└─────────────────────┘ └─────────────────────┘ └─────────────────────┘
```

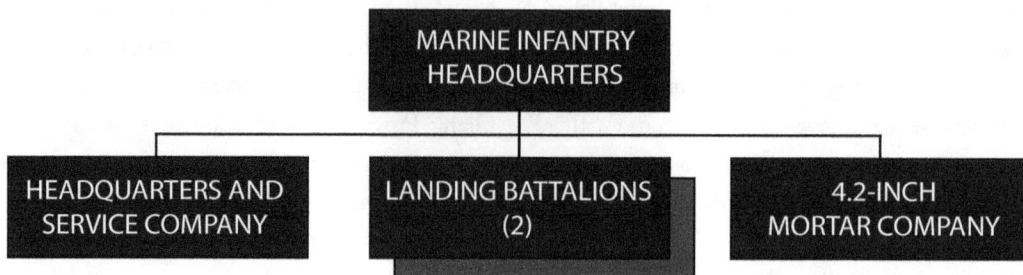

VNMC TABLE OF ORGANIZATION AS OF 18 FEBRUARY 1956
(AUTHORIZED STRENGTH 1,837)

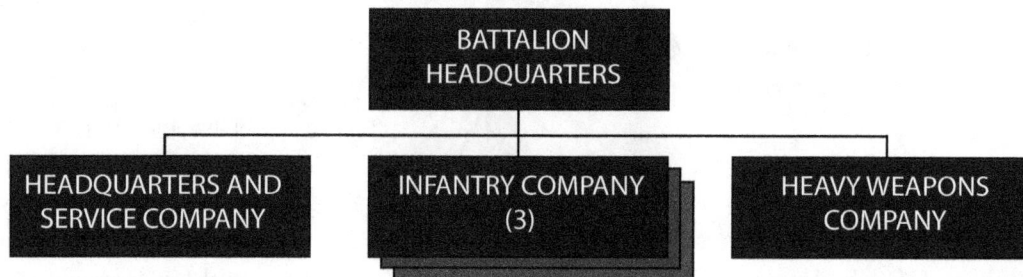

```
                    ┌─────────────────────┐
                    │      BATTALION      │
                    │    HEADQUARTERS     │
                    └─────────────────────┘
          ┌───────────────────┼───────────────────┐
┌─────────────────────┐ ┌─────────────────────┐ ┌─────────────────────┐
│   HEADQUARTERS AND  │ │  INFANTRY COMPANY   │ │    HEAVY WEAPONS    │
│   SERVICE COMPANY   │ │         (3)         │ │      COMPANY        │
└─────────────────────┘ └─────────────────────┘ └─────────────────────┘
```

LANDING BATTALION TABLE OF ORGANIZATION AS OF 18 FEBRUARY 1956
(AUTHORIZED STRENGTH 728)

In June 1956, Colonel Croizat was relieved as senior Marine advisor by Lieutenant Colonel William N. Wilkes, a World War II veteran of the Guadalcanal campaign. Colonel Wilkes held the post for the next two years. In August, President Diem temporarily elevated Captain Bui Pho Chi, who had commanded the 1st Landing Battalion during the period of political unrest in 1955, to head the Vietnamese marines. In October 1956, however, Major Le Nhu Hung, who commanded the VNMC for the next four years, replaced him.

Although the lack of a third battalion limited the VNMC's capabilities, much was accomplished between 1956 and 1959. The U.S. advisors established a formal school program for the Vietnamese officers and senior noncommissioned officers, and in 1958 Vietnamese marine officers began attending the U.S. Marine Corps' Basic School and Junior School at Quantico,

Virginia. The Marine advisors also increased emphasis on marksmanship training, and personnel and logistics problems were addressed and resolved. Assessments of improvements in tactical proficiency resulting from the advisors' efforts were, unfortunately, not possible because in this early period the advisors were required to adhere to MAAG policy prohibiting them from accompanying the units they advised into combat.

In addition to training and administrative activities, the battalions spent a considerable amount of time in the field. From December 1958 to January 1959, the 1st Landing Battalion operated against Viet Cong elements in An Xuyen, South Vietnam's southernmost province, killing a number of military and political leaders and capturing others. A few months later, both battalions were committed to field

Upon their return to South Vietnam, this group of Vietnamese marines—the first to attend the Marine Corps' Basic School at Quantico, Virginia—pose with their U.S. Marine advisors. On the extreme left is Capt Le Nguyen Khang, who became the Vietnamese Marine Corps commandant on 24 May 1960. At extreme right is Marine advisor then-Capt Michael J. Gott, and to his right is LtCol Frank R. Wilkerson Jr., the senior Marine advisor.

operations. The 1st Landing Battalion, operating with a Civil Guard unit in An Xuyen Province in May 1959, reportedly inflicted more than 200 casualties on enemy units. One company of the 2d Landing Battalion, operating in Vinh Binh Province, located south of Saigon on the seacoast, reportedly killed 18 enemy combatants and captured more than 100 others. In spite of their early successes, an effort had been made in 1958 to abolish the Vietnamese marines (a similar effort met with failure in 1956). It was disapproved. Instead, the VNMC, which had proven its worth, would continue to grow.

The successes enjoyed by the VNMC and the ARVN came at the expense of the Viet Cong cadres. These cadres consisted of Viet Minh soldiers who remained in place after the 1954 Geneva Agreement or South Vietnamese who had gone north after the 1954 partition and infiltrated back to the vicinity of their native villages after receiving training in the DRV. Between 1955 and 1958, attrition diminished the Viet Cong's ranks. The ranks of Communist Party members in South Vietnam dropped from 60,000 members in 1955 to just 5,000 in 1958. The Communist organization was making little progress in South Vietnam.

In January 1959, the Communists' fortunes began to improve when the DRV's Lao Dong Party passed a resolution to provide assistance. It had become apparent that U.S. forces intended to remain in South Vietnam for a period of undetermined length and that South Vietnam's forces were growing in size, experience, and capability. To address this deteriorating situation, Viet Cong recruiting in the south intensified, with 70–95 percent of its manpower during this period claiming indigenous roots. Infiltration down the Ho Chi Minh Trail, which began in June 1959, provided critically needed specialists and material support. During 1959, Viet Cong forces grew from an estimated 2,500 members to 5,000. By late 1960, the force had expanded to 16,000, and, by the early months of 1961, it could count between 16,000 and 19,000 members in its ranks.

Infrastructure was also developed, and the Communist cadres became more proficient. In some villages, the Viet Cong established parallel governing systems; in others, they just took over. A National Liberation Front was created in August 1960, giving the Viet Cong a united national political structure. The military structure also grew and expanded. Companies were formed and, while they were not immediately adept at combining their operations, four Viet Cong companies did join together to overrun the headquarters of the ARVN 32d Regiment in the Mekong River Delta area in January 1960. "The Communists," a close aide to President Diem told American diplomats in April 1960, "have started a major offensive in Vietnam."

In response to the increasing enemy activity, the MAAG recommended in 1959 that South Vietnam's regular military units be strengthened and expanded. It was on this recommendation that the VNMC was again enlarged. On 1 June 1959, when its two battalions returned from the field, a third landing battalion was formed and stationed at a camp adjacent to the Cuu Long Navy Yard. This battalion was formed around a nucleus of officers and noncommissioned officers taken from the two existing landing battalions, most of whom were seasoned marines and veterans of fighting against the sects and the Viet Cong. The remainder of this newly formed battalion was manned by troops transferred from the amphibious elements of the reorganized ARVN.

Further VNMC changes included the addition of a fourth rifle company to each of the three battalions, the disestablishment of the heavy weapons companies, and the establishment of 81mm mortar and 57mm recoilless rifle platoons within each battalion's headquarters and service company. New M1 rifles and other weapons, including two 60mm mortars and the personnel to man them, were added to each of the rifle companies. The final structure, formally designated the Marine Corps Group, included a group headquarters, an administration and service company, a 4.2-inch mortar battery, and the

three infantry battalions. Overall, the VNMC now totaled 2,276 officers and men.

In mid-1961, in tandem with a major increase in the Republic of Vietnam Armed Forces, the VNMC was again enlarged, this time by more than 1,000 men. A fourth infantry battalion was added to the Marine Corps Group's T/O, as was a 75mm pack-howitzer battery. The infantry battalion established its headquarters near the coastal resort town of Vung Tau, about 40 miles southeast of Saigon. The 75mm battery, consisting of ARVN artillerymen who were transferred to the VNMC, was garrisoned at Thu Duc, a small town located about 13 miles north of the capital. On 1 August 1961, the organizational chart for the Marine Corps Group included a group headquarters with a military intelligence group attached, an administration and service company, a medical company, an artillery battery, and four marine infantry battalions, for a total of 3,321 officers and enlisted men.

U.S. Marines Search for an Expanded Role

Since its inception in 1950, the MAAG in South Vietnam had continually expanded to meet the increasing support requirements levied upon it. Initially, it supported the French, but after the 1954 Geneva Conference and the partition of Vietnam at the 17th parallel, the MAAG turned its attention to supporting the RVN's military forces. In some instances, entire U.S. Army and U.S. Air Force units were committed. These commitments did not go unnoticed by the leadership of the U.S. Marine Corps.

In a 25 January 1962 letter to the CMC, Lieutenant General Alan Shapley, commanding general of the FMFPac, addressed the issue of increasing the Corps' support to South Vietnam. In his four-page, "Top Secret" letter, he argued forcefully—and made specific recommendations—for major increases to the support the Marine Corps was then providing to the RVN military. He noted that there were 2,697 U.S. military personnel serving in various advisory, combat support, and combat service support roles in the RVN and, by 31 August 1962, that number would climb to 6,202. The advisory and staff billets had largely been taken by the U.S. Army and Air Force. In addition, several complete units— three Army helicopter companies and an Air Force tactical squadron—had been deployed to the RVN. General Shapley argued that "our scale of participation should be reexamined

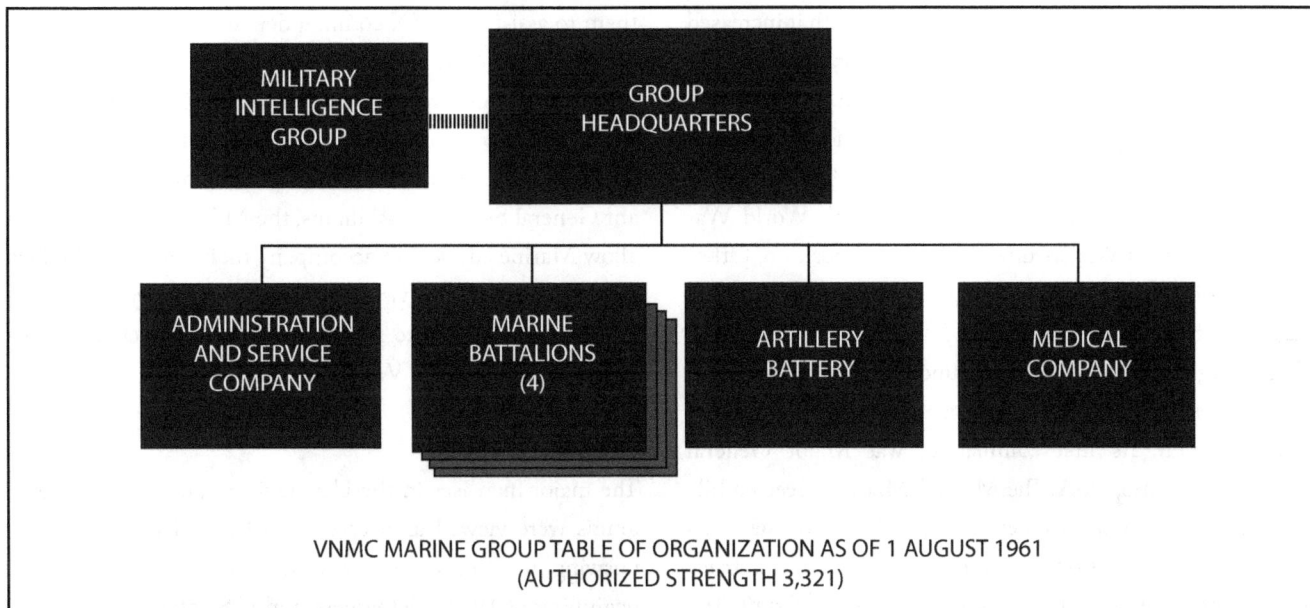

VNMC MARINE GROUP TABLE OF ORGANIZATION AS OF 1 AUGUST 1961
(AUTHORIZED STRENGTH 3,321)

on the assumption that the Marine Corps cannot afford *not* [emphasis in the original] to participate in counterguerrilla actions now being conducted in South Vietnam."

Shapley further argued that the Marine Corps' contribution should be concentrated in "a single area"—specifically I Corps in the north of South Vietnam—"where Marines are most likely to operate in the event of execution of contingency plans" and where contributions would be "positively identified." Participation by individual advisors in the MAAG program, General Shapley offered, "should be paralleled by participation by support type units of FMFPac in order to gain operational experience at the unit level." The support units that Shapley had in mind included, but were not limited to, air transportation (fixed-wing and helicopter) units. At the advisor level, he advocated providing Marine advisors to the two I Corps ARVN divisions at the corps, division, regiment, and battalion levels. The cost to the Marine Corps to support this recommendation would not be insignificant: 35 field grade officers, 65 company grade officers, and 45 enlisted personnel would be required.

General Shapley did not have to wait long to get his wish. On 8 February 1962, the United States announced a major restructuring of its military assistance program, with significant increases in manpower—including Marines. Within weeks, Shapley recommended that a full Marine medium helicopter squadron, with maintenance support units, be deployed to South Vietnam. On 15 April, Marine Medium Helicopter Squadron 362 (HMM-362) flew into Soc Trang, South Vietnam, to begin combat support operations in support of ARVN and VNMC forces. This Marine helicopter support would continue for more than two years and end only when the squadron was incorporated into the major combat forces and the Marine Corps began deploying to South Vietnam in March 1965.

It took longer for the two ARVN I Corps divisions to get their Marine advisors. As the military situation deteriorated in late 1964, however, the Marine Corps was directed to provide 60 officers and noncommissioned officers to serve as advisors to the ARVN units in I Corps. The 3d MarDiv was tasked to provide the required personnel. In mid-September, the first four advisory teams—comprising a captain, a first lieutenant, a gunnery sergeant, and a corporal radio operator—arrived in Da Nang to assume advisory duties to the two I Corps ARVN divisions.

As the RVN military grew in size, the requirement to increase the U.S. advisory and support staff also grew. On 8 February 1962, USMACV supplanted the MAAG to better manage the rapidly increasing support demands. General Paul D. Harkins, USA, assumed command and, in his capacity as a subunified commander in the Pacific Theater, reported directly to Admiral Harry D. Felt, USN, the Commander in Chief, Pacific (CinCPac), whose headquarters was in Hawaii.

The establishment of USMACV brought with it increased billets and responsibilities for Marines. Twenty-one staff billets in the new USMACV T/O were allocated to the Marine Corps. At the most senior level, the chief of staff position would be filled by a Marine Corps major general. Major General Richard G. Weede, a veteran of both World War II and the Korean War, assumed this pivotal position. Other Marines joined the USMACV staff as deputy chief of staff, J-2, and as branch chiefs in the J-3, J-4, J-5, and J-6 divisions.

A reorganized MAAG, now subordinate to USMACV, assumed responsibility for the advisory aspects of the assistance program. Its first commander was Major General Charles J. Timmes, USA. The MAAG Marines received billets that included deputy chief of staff and head of the plans branch of the J-3 division. A future modification of the structure elevated a Marine to the position of chief of staff. The first Marine to serve in this capacity was Colonel Earl E. Anderson, who later became the Assistant Commandant of the Marine Corps.

The Advisory Force Grows

The MAAG T/O provided for a dramatic change in the size and responsibilities of the Marine advisory effort. The new organization called for the establishment of an 18-man Marine Advisory Division subordinate to the Navy section, with the military occupational specialty (MOS) for each advisor matching the functions of his advisory duties. A lieutenant colonel continued to act as the senior Marine advisor, with a major serving as both the assistant senior advisor and artillery advisor. Six captains were assigned: four infantry battalion advisors, one engineer advisor, and one supply advisor. A master sergeant filled the position of first sergeant, and three gunnery sergeants were assigned as advisors for small unit training, artillery assistance, and communications. Four staff sergeants with a logistics MOS assisted the infantry battalion officers, and one staff sergeant served as the motor transport advisor. A sergeant handled administrative responsibilities. By May 1962, all of these billets had been filled.

Many policy changes, including a major change in the advisory program, accompanied the increases in staffing. Most significant was the January 1962 authorization from Admiral Harry Felt, the CinCPac, allowing U.S. advisors to accompany the units they advised into combat. This would allow

them to assist the RVN commanders in operations, communications, resupply, and other areas. It was not well known at the time, but two years earlier, in 1960, the then-senior Marine advisor, Lieutenant Colonel Frank R. Wilkerson, had requested and received informal permission from Lieutenant General Samuel T. Williams, the MAAG commander, to allow Marine advisors to accompany their units into the field as nonparticipating advisors. In this capacity, they became the first U.S. servicemen to actively participate in actual combat operations against the Viet Cong.

Viet Cong in 1962

The major increases in the U.S. advisory and assistance programs were viewed as necessary in light of the recognized upswing in Viet Cong strength and capabilities. At the beginning of 1962, Vietnamese and U.S. intelligence sources believed that Viet Cong military forces in South Vietnam—both full and part time—totaled approximately 25,000 men. The U.S. categorized these as "main forces," "local forces," and "village activists," depending on their functions and composition. The real strength of the Viet Cong resided in the main forces, thought to number about 9,000 troops. These were divided into 20 small battalions and several independent companies and were capable of executing interprovincial operations. They consisted mainly of North Vietnamese troops or South Vietnamese citizens who had trained in North Vietnam and had returned. Next in capability and structure were the 8,000 part-time, but well trained, local forces. They were organized into companies and platoons and operated independently within their local districts. At the bottom of the structure—but still considered very valuable—were 8,000 village activists. They were part-time guerrillas who worked the rice paddies during the day and conducted military operations at night. Often they were the male members of a village who were too young or too old to serve in a main force or local force unit. While their contributions as fighters might be minimal, they proved to be excellent sources of intelligence information and often served as porters and guides for main force units operating in their province.

Recognizing the war as a principally political—as opposed to a military—struggle, the combat activities of the Viet Cong's military forces were carefully coordinated with the Communists' political operations. The Central Office for

Vietnamese marines attack from a concealed position during a search operation on the Ca Mau Peninsula, south of Saigon, in the summer of 1962. HMM-362—"Archie's Angels"—supported this operation.

South Vietnam effected coordination at the highest level. This office, thought to be located in Binh Duong Province to the northeast of Saigon, was responsible for orchestrating all Communist activities throughout South Vietnam. Central Office leaders divided the country into six military regions that were further divided into provinces and districts, not unlike the structure utilized by the South Vietnamese government. At each level, a small but highly disciplined Communist political committee integrated the activities of its military forces with the actions of its political forces, while ensuring that all activities were in concert with those of its senior headquarters. By the beginning of 1962, the Communists in South Vietnam—who had been actively subverting the South Vietnamese government since 1954—were well entrenched and operating in phase II of Mao Tse-tung's three-phase insurgent plan. In some locations in South Vietnam, they were poised to move into phase III.

Marines in Action

The VNMC expanded once again in 1962. On 1 January, it received authorization to increase to 5,482 officers and men.

With its growth, the Marine Corps Group added new units and was redesignated the Vietnamese Marine Brigade. The number of infantry battalions remained unchanged at four; however, two new battalions—one artillery and one amphibious support—were added. The artillery battalion included one battery with eight 105mm howitzers, two batteries of eight 75mm pack-howitzers, and a headquarters and service battery. The amphibious support unit of 1,038 officers and men provided the brigade with reconnaissance, communications, motor transport, medical, engineering, and training support. To reflect the fact that the brigade was now training all of its recruits, a recruit training section was also added to the T/O. Lieutenant Colonel Le Nguyen Khang, who had replaced Major Le Nhu Hung as the marines' commander on 24 May 1960, continued as the Commandant of the Vietnamese Marine Brigade.

With their expanded numbers, the U.S. Marine advisors were able to participate in every VNMC combat operation undertaken in 1962. Their support included operational planning and planning for the employment of supporting arms. If an amphibious operation was planned, the Marine advisors

U.S. Marine advisors to the Vietnamese Marine Corps relax on board the USS *Perch* (APSS 313) prior to the start of an amphibious landing exercise south of Da Nang. From left are GySgt Levi W. Wood, Capt James McWilliams, and Capt William J. P. Mannix.

coordinated with their U.S. Navy counterparts who were advising the Vietnamese Navy. Given the VNMC officers' limited experience with helicopter operations, the Marine advisors often found themselves coordinating their units' helilifts as well.

Building a sense of trust with their often-senior counterparts was imperative to the success of the U.S. Marines' advisory role. However, given the Marines' relative lack of experience in counterinsurgency and jungle warfare, offering tactical advice to Vietnamese officers, who in some cases had been fighting Communist guerrillas since the French-Indochina War, often proved a challenge that required tact, patience, and subtle persuasive powers. To build this intangible yet critically important trust and mutual understanding, the Marine advisors stayed with their units in the field and shared the same meals, dangers, and discomforts. The senior Marine advisors viewed "continuous association with the Vietnamese marines as the single most essential ingredient to a successful advisory program."

The VNMC participated in 23 combat operations in 1962, 12 of which included amphibious landings and 8 of which were heliborne assaults. The types of missions varied widely from security duty around key government installations to assaults—amphibious or heliborne—on suspected

Viet Cong base camps. Typical was the extended operation undertaken by the VNMC's 2d Battalion early in the year. Assigned to the provincial chief of An Xuyen Province, South Vietnam's southernmost province, the battalion operated continually from 18 February until 26 April. With Captain Evan L. Parker assigned as the advisor, the battalion conducted a heliborne landing, provided troop escorts for numerous truck convoys, and fought several minor engagements with the Viet Cong. Based on Captain Parker's count—which varied considerably from that of his Vietnamese battalion commander—the two months of operations resulted in 40 Viet Cong killed and another 20 wounded.

The 1st Battalion, advised by Captain Bradley S. Snell, served as the reserve force for the II Corps commander. Although prepared to react to enemy threats, the battalion was assigned security duty for government installations. As the corps reserve, it conducted a heliborne assault and several search missions. During one of the search missions, the battalion discovered and destroyed a Viet Cong small arms factory. Statistically, however, the 1st Battalion's four-month stay in II Corps reflected very little in the way of positive results. The battalion accounted for only 4 Viet Cong dead and 1 wounded, while 16 of their own were killed and 28 wounded, many due to sniper fire.

The 4th Battalion was activated in midyear with Captain Donald R. Christensen as its Marine advisor. Its first combat assignment came during the first week of August when it joined the 43d ARVN Infantry Regiment in an attempt to locate and destroy Communist forces that were operating in the vicinity of Phan Thiet, the capital of Binh Thuan Province, located on the coast some 95 miles from Saigon. It was supported in this operation by Battery A of the VNMC Artillery Battalion. When the operation concluded on 22 August, the battalion reverted to the control of the province chief who employed it in clearing and resettlement operations. During this deployment, the battalion resettled approximately 600 civilians in support of the national government's Strategic Hamlet Program.

As 1962 drew to a close, the Vietnamese Marine Brigade had little to show in the way of accomplishments. It had conducted no truly major operations, and because its battalions were employed as independent units, the brigade headquarters had gained no experience in the conduct of multibattalion operations. Further, the brigade's supporting amphibious and artillery battalions had received no meaningful employment. In an accurate, but not complimentary, assessment of the brigade's employment, Major Alfred J. Croft, the assistant senior Marine advisor, noted that the province chiefs tended to misuse the marine units by assigning them unproductive missions, such as static security. In 1962, at least, that was certainly the case.

Counterinsurgency Focus

In the intensifying conflict in South Vietnam, General Shapley saw an opportunity to involve additional Marines and, in the process, increase their skills and knowledge in counterinsurgency warfare. Early in 1961, he signed off on a program that detailed company grade officers and staff noncommissioned officers to 30 days of temporary duty as observers with South Vietnamese military units. Beginning in May 1961, the OJT Program began assigning small numbers of Marines from the various FMFPac commands—but principally from the 3d MarDiv and the 1st MAW—to temporary assigned duty to observe the counterguerrilla tactics being developed and employed in the RVN. Although tours were brief, over time the program built a small cadre of junior officers and

Defense Department (Marine Corps) A410929

Capt James McWilliams takes some time prior to the start of an amphibious operation to instruct 2dLt Nguyen Viet Bach in the techniques of long-distance rowing. Bach was the commanding officer of the Marine Amphibious Support Battalion's Reconnaissance Company, the first Vietnamese unit to be trained in amphibious reconnaissance.

staff noncommissioned officers with at least a passing familiarity with counterinsurgency operations, in general, and the deteriorating situation in South Vietnam, in particular.

The senior leadership of the Okinawa-based 3d MarDiv recognized the seriousness of the situation and the possibility for the employment of large numbers of Marines. In early 1961, Major General Donald M. Weller, the division commander, began to shift his division's planning and training efforts away from a strictly conventional, amphibious orientation to counterguerrilla operations. He directed his staff to "turn the entire orientation of the division toward the type of intervention [which] we would be faced with in Southeast Asia." Although General Weller relinquished command of the 3d MarDiv in September 1961, his successor, Major General Robert E. Cushman, continued the focus on counterinsurgency operations. In October 1961, moving forward with Weller's initiative, Cushman convened a Counterguerrilla Warfare Study Group to address counterinsurgency issues.

The purpose of the study group was "to formulate a division guerrilla warfare training program." The group consisted of three officers: Major James W. Wood, a graduate of the Counterinsurgency School at Fort Bragg, North Carolina; Major Richard B. Twohey; and First Lieutenant Gene A. Deegan, both of whom were graduates of the Jungle Warfare School in Johore, Malaya. In its report, the study group recommended the establishment of two training courses. Both were quickly developed and training soon began. An eight-day Infantry Unit Course trained rifle companies for operations against guerrillas in a jungle environment. The training was conducted in Okinawa's junglelike Northern Training Area and included instruction on the historical background of guerrilla warfare; the individual guerrilla, his habits, and methods of operation; current guerrilla operations in Southeast Asia; and the Marine Corps' role in guerrilla warfare.

The training program concluded with a two-and-a-half day platoon-size exercise, during which each of the rifle company's platoons conducted a hunt for guerrillas in the area's jungle environment against an "actual" guerrilla force. The second course, a one-day Staff and Command Course, focused on battalion-level staffs and included five hours of lectures and a two-and-a-half hour map exercise. The course was designed to standardize the battalion staff members' knowledge of guerrilla operations, prepare them to employ companies that had completed the Infantry Unit Course, and prepare them to train their units for guerrilla operations.

The FMFPac OJT Program and the 3d MarDiv training program complemented each other in several ways. While the OJT Program enhanced the knowledge of counterguerrilla operations for individual officers and staff noncommissioned officers, the division's courses provided a similar exposure to counterguerrilla operations for platoons, rifle companies, and battalion-level staffs. Moreover, officers and staff noncommissioned officers returning from the OJT Program enhanced the division's training by providing assistance in planning and supervising the training programs.

In December 1961, Lieutenant Deegan, who had arrived on Okinawa with a transplacement battalion the previous May, received orders for the OJT Program and was sent on temporary additional duty (TAD) to South Vietnam. His experiences and observations, in large measure, mirror those of the other Marines who participated in the OJT Program at this time. After orientation briefings from the Marine advisors on the USMACV staff, Deegan was assigned to a base northwest of Saigon where he assumed duties as a small unit tactics instructor (translators were employed to minimize the language barrier for South Vietnamese units). The days were uneventful, and the enemy threat proved to be minimal. Approximately halfway through his tour, Lieutenant Deegan was transferred to an ARVN unit located at Ca Mau in the Mekong Delta south of Saigon. Advised by U.S. Army officers, to whom Deegan believed he was both a "burden and a bother," this unit had a more operational flavor.

There were some minor firefights, but actual combat was very limited and there were no night operations. The ARVN and the Popular Force (local militia) units entered villages before dark and remained there until the next morning. This was not their only deficiency. The Vietnamese soldiers, Lieutenant Deegan observed, did not see themselves as being in the "winning hearts and minds business." Typically, he noted,

an army unit would come into a village and "take over," and the village inhabitants "hosted" the unit whether they wanted to or not.

Once outside of Saigon, it was evident that a Communist threat was evolving and an insurgency was building. "There was a war to be fought," Deegan observed, "but nobody was fighting it." That said, he cited three benefits that accrued from his TAD, which stretched to nearly 45 days. First, his exposure to actual counterinsurgency operations improved his self-esteem. Second, it gained him increased credibility with his fellow Marines. Finally, the lessons learned aided him in training and fighting with his company when he commanded Company F, 2d Battalion, 1st Marines, in I Corps in 1966 and 1967.

Thailand: Operation Millpond, 1961

The Geneva Agreement signed on 20 July 1954 called for an independent and democratically governed Laos. However, events on the ground between the end of World War II and mid-1954 made it clear that such an outcome for this land-locked nation, slightly larger than the state of Idaho and containing approximately two million people, was very unlikely. Strategically located in the middle of Southeast Asia, Laos's neighbors to the north and east were the People's Republic of China and the DRV. Its remaining neighbors in 1954 included South Vietnam to the east, Cambodia to the south, Thailand to the south and west, and Burma to the west. The key to subverting these four non-Communist countries was control of Laos. It was an unfortunate fact of geography that Laos was destined to become a pawn in the Cold War, the initial step in the Soviet Union's, China's, and North Vietnam's efforts to drive the United States out of the Far East and bring all of the Southeast Asian nations and Burma under Communist rule.

The contest for the allegiance of Laos and its government began in the late 1940s. In 1949, Laos became an independent state within the French Union, and in 1953 (as French fortunes continued to decline) France recognized Laos as a fully independent and sovereign nation. The United States, England, and France extended diplomatic recognition in February 1950, and most of the free-world nations followed suit. In 1955, Laos was admitted to the United Nations.

In the period before Laotian independence, the French had encountered resistance to their return from forces

Mainland Southeast Asia

TROPIC OF CANCER

CHINA

BURMA

NORTH VIETNAM

LAOS

HANOI

GULF OF TONKIN

HAINAN

VIENTIANE

RANGOON

THAILAND

BANGKOK

SOUTH VIETNAM

CAMBODIA

PHNOM PENH

SAIGON

GULF OF THAILAND

ANDAMAN SEA

SOUTH CHINA SEA

N

MALAYSIA

KUALA LUMPUR

SINGAPORE

SUMATRA

EQUATOR

★ NATIONAL CAPITAL

MILES

0   100   200   300

0   100   200   300   400

KILOMETERS

affiliated with a provisional "Free Lao" government. As the French reestablished control, much of the leadership of the Free Lao forces—including many members of the royal family—fled to Thailand. Following independence in 1949, most returned to Vientiane (the seat of the administrative government) or Luang Prabang (the royal capital) and began to form a government. One royal family member—Prince Souphanouvong—traveled north and east to join with Ho Chi Minh, who was establishing the Communist-sponsored and Communist-controlled DRV. The following September, the DRV radio station announced the formation of the Pathet Lao, a resistance government. In the months that followed, the resistance government elected Prince Souphanouvong as its prime minister and established a Laotion National United Front and a People's Liberation Army. There was little doubt that the North Vietnamese Communists could claim paternity.

Sporadic guerrilla activity along the Laos–North Vietnam border marked both 1951 and 1952, but during this period Laos itself remained relatively free of active fighting. This, of course, was not the case to the east in Vietnam where the Viet Minh forces of Ho Chi Minh were engaging the French with forces up to division strength. The situation in Laos took a serious turn for the worse in April 1953, when Prince Souphanouvong and his Pathet Lao forces—supported by combat-hardened Viet Minh veterans—launched a full-scale invasion and quickly took control of the two northern provinces of Sam Neua and Phong Saly. Efforts by the Royal Laotian Government to dislodge the Pathet Lao forces ended in failure.

The April–July 1954 conference held in Geneva, Switzerland, produced agreements that were designed to end all of the fighting in Indochina. Specifically for Laos, the agreements provided for a cease-fire arrangement that would bring about the integration of the two Pathet Lao–held provinces into the national government. To supervise the execution of the Geneva Agreement, an international commission with representatives from Canada, India, and Poland was established with its headquarters in Vientiane. The Pathet Lao initially refused to participate in elections and steadfastly rebuffed all attempts by the national government to reassert control over the provinces of Sam Neua and Phong Saly. In 1958, they did participate in elections, and although the pro-government candidates won a resounding victory, the Pathet Lau were able to elect more than 10 of their supporters.

In the end, the Geneva Agreement did little to foster democracy in Laos. In fact, it had just the opposite effect. By recognizing all political parties, the agreement conferred legality, respectability, and prestige on the Laotian Communist leaders. The Communist Party—the Neo Lao Had Xat—gained status as a legitimate party, positioning it to employ its trained and disciplined Pathet Lao cadres. Its tactics, until fighting escalated in late summer 1960, focused on infiltration, subversion, and preparation.

In August 1960, a chain of events began that eventually brought the United States into active involvement in an attempt to keep Laos from falling into the Communist camp. During that month, a paratroop battalion commanded by a little-known captain, Kong Le, took control of the capital of Vientiane and passed the reigns of government to Prince Souvanna Phouma, a royal family member favorably disposed to the Pathet Lao. The first actions of Souvanna Phouma's self-proclaimed "neutralist" government were to invite the Soviet Union to open an embassy in Laos and to pledge to maintain friendly relations with North Vietnam and China. The following four months witnessed a steady increase in Communist influence in the government, until late in the year when the army, under former defense minister General Phoumi Nosavan, retook the city. After losing it for a short period, the army again retook Vientiane and, in mid-December, expelled the Communist forces. The fighting, however, was not over.

As the Pathet Lao and Kong Le's forces were being pushed back to the east, reports began to surface that they were receiving substantial support from North Vietnam and the Soviet Union. As this support—which was reported to include weapons, related war materials, and North Vietnamese troops—continued to pour in, resistance in areas held by Communist forces stiffened. In early January 1961, Communist China's Radio Beijing reported that the Pathet Lao and Kong Le's forces had taken control of the strategic Plain of Jars, including the town of Xiengkhouang and its airfield. From this position, they could threaten the administrative capital of Vientiane and the royal capital of Luang Prabang.

The United States had been aiding the Laos government—some $300 million had been provided by the beginning of

1960—since the signing of the Geneva Agreement. The aid had gone to support the Royal Lao Army, the police, and other governmental services. In 1960, the limited military assistance program in Laos was being administered by a small program evaluation office. Staffed mostly by technicians, the principal focus of the office was on training the Laotian Army's personnel in the technical and maintenance aspects of the equipment being provided. They lacked any capability to provide training or advisory support. In fact, tactical training remained under the cognizance of French military units. As the Laotian military faltered and the Pathet Lao forces gained strength and threatened to overrun the entire country, the United States—its assistance clearly inadequate—was confronted with the task of reversing this unfavorable flow of events. As the Dwight D. Eisenhower administration left office in January 1961, the decision for an appropriate course of action passed to the new and untested John F. Kennedy administration.

President Kennedy Commits U.S. Forces

In March 1961, Admiral Felt briefed President Kennedy on the Laotian situation and the U.S. Pacific force levels available to address it. U.S. pilots, under contract to the Laotian government, had been flying resupply and troop transport missions employing four U.S.-made helicopters and aging Douglas C-47 Skytrain transports. They had sustained several hits on their aircraft, and as the level of fighting increased, their support had become increasingly inadequate. A U.S. embassy C-47 aircraft conducting an observation mission had been shot down by hostile fire with the loss of all seven crewmembers—the first U.S. casualties of the Laotian conflict.

The president quickly recognized that action was urgently required to reverse this deteriorating situation. His plan called for increasing the support being provided to the pro-Western forces in Laos through the employment of increased numbers of nonmilitary helicopters and fixed-wing transport aircraft flown by U.S.—but nonmilitary (Air America)—pilots. Until the operation could become self-sustaining, U.S. military personnel—specifically Marines—who were trained in aircraft maintenance, flight line operations, and related functions would provide support. These U.S. military forces would be stationed in northeast Thailand, approximately 40 miles south of the Laotian administrative capital of Vientiane.

Order to Deploy Marine Corps Forces

At approximately 0200 on Sunday, 12 March 1961, MABS-16, located at the Marine Corps Air Facility (MCAF) in Futema, Okinawa,* received its first message alerting it for possible deployment on what would become Operation Millpond. The message directed the squadron to be prepared with 48-hours notice to move by theater airlift a reinforced Marine Corps Aviation Squadron with supplies, equipment, and personnel to Udorn, Thailand, and establish an expeditionary base for operations and field maintenance for 20 Sikorsky HUS-1 Seahorse helicopters. The deployment was to be completed within six days of receiving the order to execute. The initial requirement to establish and maintain a 30-day level of spare parts for the helicopters was changed to a 120-day supply prior to deployment.

Originally, MABS-16 envisioned deploying with a total of 455 personnel, but a U.S. State Department–Royal Thai Government conference imposed a ceiling of 300 as the maximum number of Marines that would be allowed to deploy to Thailand. With the exceptions of petroleum, oil, and lubricants that would be supplied by rail from Bangkok, Thailand, and subsistence support after 10 days, which would be provided by the Navy commissary store in Bangkok, MABS-16 would be self-sustaining with expeditionary equipment. In addition to the camp equipment required to support its Marines, MABS-16 was directed to deploy with additional camp equipment to support 80 Air America personnel.

In addition to organic personnel and equipment, the following seven detachments also deployed in support of MABS-16:

- Detachment, Headquarters and Maintenance Squadron 16 that was responsible for maintaining a Class "C" and "D" aircraft maintenance facility;

- Detachment, Marine Air Base Squadron 17 that was responsible for setting up and maintaining a tactical airfield fuel dispensing system (TAFDS) and an air freight facility, and for supporting the crew of a Marine Douglas R4D-8 Skytrain transport;

---

*Marine Corps Air Facility Futema, Okinawa, was activated on 1 January 1960. It was redesignated as Marine Corps Air Station (Helicopter) Futema on 1 June 1970, and redesignated again as Marine Corps Air Station (Helicopter) Futenma on 22 March 1976. Its current designation (as of 2014) is Marine Corps Air Station Futenma.

Air Force transport planes from the Military Air Transport Command brought many of the Marines and their equipment to the airfield at Udorn, Thailand.

- Detachment, Communications Company, 3d MarDiv;

- Infantry Platoon, 3d Marine Regiment, 3d MarDiv;

- Engineer Platoon, 3d Pioneer Battalion, 7th Engineer Regiment;

- Marine Aircraft Tactical Control Unit-1 (-) (MATCU-1; and

- Detachment, Marine Wing Headquarters Group 1 that was responsible for communications and postal support.

The execute order for Operation Millpond (the operational name assigned to the MABS-16 deployment), which was received on Sunday, 19 March 1961, directed movement to commence on Wednesday, 22 March, with the airlift phase to be completed in four days. The order further directed MABS-16 to be prepared to receive helicopters on Monday, 27 March, and to begin supporting helicopter operations immediately thereafter, as directed by appropriate authority. Nine aircraft—five Lockheed C-130 Hercules and four Douglas C-124 Globemasters—were scheduled to depart Okinawa on the evening of 22 March and arrive at Udorn the next day. Intermediate stops were planned at Clark Air Base in the Philippines and Don Muang Airport outside Bangkok. Both organic 1st MAW and U.S. Air Force 315th Air Division aircraft were tasked to participate. Due to mechanical issues, only seven of these aircraft made it to Udorn on 23 March.

MABS-16's Mission

MABS-16's mission, in part, read: "When directed, MABS-16 (Rein[forced]) deploy to Udorn . . . for purposes of establishing an expeditionary base for operation and flight maintenance of 20 HUS-1 helicopters." In fact, its mission demanded much more from its 300-man force.

The squadron was to provide total aircraft maintenance and airfield services, plus training in both areas, and other support to Air America, which had been publicly identified as a company under contract with the U.S. government. An April 1961 *New York Times* article described Air America as

a "subsidiary of Civil Air Transport, a private company based in Taiwan." In fact, it was a company covertly operated by the Central Intelligence Agency. Under its contract, Air America provided pilots, aircrew members, executives, administrative support, and other personnel. The company, however, was initially unable to perform the maintenance on its aircraft to keep them flightworthy, and it could not satisfactorily manage airfield operations. It was expected that after a period of training by the MABS-16 aircraft maintenance and airfield services Marines, Air America personnel would assume full responsibility for the maintenance of their helicopters and airfield operations. At that point, MABS-16 would have accomplished its mission and would terminate operations and return to its home base on Okinawa.

As previously noted, Air America pilots had already been flying missions with four HUS-1s in Laos since December 1960, under control of the program evaluation office. One had been lost to enemy fire, and all of the others had been hit by enemy fire. Under its new and expanded contract, Air America was to grow to 20 HUS-1 helicopters, all to be received from the U.S. government. It was to operate these aircraft in support of the Royal Laotian forces engaged in combat operations against Pathet Lao insurgents that were being supported by North Vietnamese ground troops and supplied by the Soviet Union and China.

Of the 16 additional aircraft made available, 13 flew into the Udorn airfield on 27 March. Although efforts had been made to "sanitize" the aircraft of any military markings, when the sun struck the fuselage of the arriving HUS-1s, a large white star and the word "Marines" were clearly visible under the light coat of green paint that had been applied to each helicopter. With the arrival of the final 3 helicopters a few days later and the repair of the 3 that had been provided the previous December, Air America had 19 operational aircraft. The loss of a second aircraft a short time later left it with 18 assigned as April approached.

Because maintaining Air America's operational capability was a priority for MABS-16, among the first Marines to arrive at Udorn were 2 officers and 30 enlisted Marines from Headquarters and Maintenance Squadron 16's aircraft maintenance detachment. They immediately set about establishing aircraft repair shops in an empty hanger adjacent to the airfield. Camp construction crews also arrived early. Communications was also a priority, and by 23 March several communicators had arrived. Over the next few days, the remainder of the force was flown in.

"No Comment"

During the first days of the operation, Lieutenant Colonel Richard W. Johnson, MABS-16's commanding officer, led an early morning all-hands meeting. At this meeting, he briefed the Marines on the command's activities and how important the command's mission was. He emphasized at every meeting that the unit's mission was not classified; however, Marines were not to talk about it with anyone. He noted that Secretary of Defense Robert S. McNamara had issued a directive making it unequivocally clear that the only comment Marines were allowed to make was "no comment."

This guidance did not sit well with the major news and television correspondents who began arriving from Laos on the evening of 23 March after learning that U.S. Marines

A considerable amount of rain falls in northeast Thailand during the monsoon season. The airfield is at the top of the photograph, and the initial, temporary camp was located to the right of the airfield.

had landed at Udorn. One correspondent reporting for the *Evening Star*, a Washington, DC, newspaper, wrote, "The Marines have landed in Thailand with their eyes open and their mouths firmly shut." As the airfield and adjacent areas were Thai property, the Marines had no authority to restrict any correspondent's access. Therefore, over the next few days, they mingled among the silent Marines in their attempts to get information. By 27 March, most of the media had become discouraged and returned to Laos. Their departure caused them to miss the story and pictures that they most coveted—the arrival of the helicopters—which took place on 28 March. On that day, there were no correspondents or photographers near the Marines' camp or the airfield.

The local Thai population was also curious about what was taking place at the airfield just down the road from their town. For the several days during and after the Marines' arrival, local citizens, often numbering in the hundreds, would arrive and stand on the main road adjacent to the airfield, observing the Marines as they erected their tent camp.

Air America's helicopters arrive for duty. Beneath the light coat of green paint, a large white star and the word "Marines" were clearly visible.

The First Weeks

The aircraft maintenance department's Marines faced a daunting dual mission. They were tasked with providing aircraft and flight line maintenance and operations for 20 HUS-1 helicopters with an anticipated utilization factor of

Photo courtesy of the author

The first Marines to arrive had to erect their own billeting and work spaces.

approximately 120 hours a month. While performing these functions—for a period expected to last for 90 to 120 days, but which in fact ran for more than six months—they were also tasked to train Air America maintenance crews that would gradually phase in and assume all aspects of aircraft maintenance and line functions. Further, the Marines of the maintenance department were tasked with maintaining all shop and test equipment, special support equipment, aircraft spares, tools, and general aircraft consumables in sufficient quantities to sustain operations.

The forced reduction of MABS-16's authorized personnel strength from the desired 455 to 300 ensured that the aircraft maintenance department was staffed to only spartan levels. To accomplish all of their tasks, only 2 officers, including 1 avionics officer, and 37 enlisted men were assigned from Headquarters and Maintenance Squadron 16 to perform the aircraft maintenance functions. Wisely, in light of the requirement to train Air America personnel, care was taken to assign experienced and qualified staff noncommissioned officers.

Within two weeks, Air America provided approximately 40 men to begin training with the Marine aircraft and flight line maintenance crews. About 15 were assigned to shops or other hanger functions. Unfortunately, as the tempo of operations picked up and backup helicopter crew chiefs were

needed for flight operations into Laos, some of these men became unavailable for maintenance training. In the early weeks, Air America's maintenance training focused principally on the flight line servicing of incoming and outgoing aircraft.

Camp Construction

Construction of the camp began immediately upon arrival and proceeded in two phases. The first dealt with the temporary camp that was built directly on the ground. An area was selected and marked off, and as tents arrived they were put up in predesignated areas. First priority was given to billeting. Once living areas had been established, the mess hall, sick bay, and office tents were put up. In approximately three weeks, the temporary camp had been completed. It served MABS-16's Marines for more than two months until a more permanent—and more livable—cantonment was constructed on the opposite side of the airfield.

The second phase—construction of the permanent camp that encompassed an area of approximately eight acres that was relatively flat and free of vegetation—took about 11 weeks to complete. The work was done by the engineer platoon, which had 1 officer and 21 enlisted Marines. When actual construction began, 1st MAW provided an additional 21 carpenters. Plans were drawn up to build the entire camp elevated above ground as it was anticipated that the entire area would be underwater when the rainy monsoon season began in the late spring.

Three buildings—all in serious states of disrepair—existed in the area chosen for the camp. These buildings were completely renovated and put into service. One building became the squadron's mess hall after all internal partitions had been removed and the building had been screened. Storage areas were constructed on both ends of this building by extending the existing decks and enclosing them. The second building was rehabilitated and turned into office and work spaces. It had room to house the sick bay, post office, exchange, squadron office, communications switchboard, and motor transport office. A dry stores warehouse was also located in this building. The third building was assigned to Air America for its office spaces.

Five platforms—on approximately 6-foot posts placed at 8-foot intervals and sunk 30 inches into the ground—were

In the initial camp, all tents—including the Squadron Aid Station pictured—were pitched on the ground, providing no protection from flooding.

erected in the main camp area. The two largest platforms were 258 feet in length and 40 feet wide and could accommodate 13 strongback general purpose tents. These were constructed in such a manner that all of the sides could be rolled up when the weather permitted. Two smaller platforms accommodated five strongback general purpose tents on one, and the camp's laundry and bath unit were placed on the other. The final platform was built to accommodate two corrugated-roofed buildings. Inside of each of these buildings, a strongback command-post tent was erected. These two buildings were joined and served as the squadron's command center.

A washhouse was also constructed and could accommodate up to 40 Marines at a time with running water provided from a gravity-fed 3,000-gallon water tank. Individual racks were constructed at each station, which allowed a Marine to insert his helmet that served as his "sink." Several heads were constructed behind the billeting area. All of the platforms and heads were connected by walkways, each of which had a removable section to allow emergency fire or ambulance vehicles to drive through the camp.

Approximately a quarter-million board feet of lumber—all rough mahogany—were used in the construction along with corrugated tin, screen, and nails. All was purchased locally at a cost of approximately $22,000. The permanent cantonment was ready and occupied before the monsoon rains began. The

elevated wooden flooring and screened-in billets were a welcome change from living on the ground with the tent flaps always down.

Logistics

MABS-16 deployed with 44 pieces of rolling stock, including M21 2 1/2-ton trucks, M38A1 1/4-ton trucks (Jeeps), M7 water trailers or "water buffaloes," MB-5 aviation

The squadron mess hall was located in one of the existing structures that had been rehabilitated by the engineers. It was built up off of the ground to prevent flooding during the monsoon season.

During the monsoon rains, the ground below the elevated cantonment was frequently flooded. The rehabilitated original building on the left housed the squadron's administration offices. Strongback tents were erected in the permanent camp, which was built entirely off the ground for flood protection. At right are strongback billeting tents.

crash-and-rescue fire trucks, and a Caterpillar D-4 crawler tractor with dozer blade. Given the extremes of the monsoon's dry and wet seasons, all rolling stock required special care. During the dry season, the roads were covered with a fine powdery dust to a depth of two to three inches, which required changing the oil in the air cleaners twice a week and lubricating all vehicles weekly. During the rainy season, particularly in August and September, all vehicles continually traveled or stood in water, often above their axles. To keep them operational, they were lubricated twice a week. Despite close attention to these problems, many drive shaft universals, wheel bearings, and brake cylinders and linings required replacement at the end of the rainy season in October. Further, the radiators on the generators that provided power to the cantonment rusted and gummed up more frequently than the radiators on the vehicles and required frequent flushing to prevent the generators from overheating.

Food service operations throughout the deployment were exceptional. After only 10 days on C rations, a galley was established in a fly tent, and three general purpose tents were outfitted to serve as the dining hall. Packaged operational B rations with a fresh food supplement were served initially. Soon thereafter, fresh food substitutions for the B rations became available through the Navy commissary in Bangkok. Dry stores were transported from Bangkok by rail, and fresh

food arrived at Udorn on MABS-16's R4D-8 aircraft. On 29 April, the engineers completed work on the abandoned building that had been designated as the squadron mess hall, and it opened for business. Complete with refrigeration, storage space, galley, mess deck, and a dry stores warehouse, this new mess hall was operated by a mess management chief, six cooks, and one baker (and after early May, several indigenous mess men), and it served three meals daily for the duration of the operation.

The acquisition of water and ice proved to be a unique, but not insurmountable, problem for the deployed force. Filtered, not potable, water was used in the camp's showers and laundry. Although not suitable for drinking, it was available in unlimited supply and was inexpensive to purchase from the town of Udorn.

To provide water suitable for drinking, a water point was established at the edge of a pond about three-quarters of a mile from the camp. The unlimited supply from the pond was processed into potable water and distributed to the mess hall and the many 400-gallon water buffaloes that were placed throughout the camp. MABS-16 did not lack for water at any time during its stay in Thailand.

The mess hall, which used large amounts of ice in its daily operations, required special consideration. Locally produced ice could not be used because it was made from unpurified water. After several visits to the local icehouse, the Marines were successful in acquiring three large ice freezing cans on a temporary basis. These cans were taken back to the camp where they were scrubbed, chlorinated, marked with an identifying paint, and then returned to the icehouse, along with a water buffalo containing potable water. The ice freezing cans were then filled, and the water was frozen. The Marines reached an agreement with the icehouse staff that the resulting blocks of ice would be sold only to the Marines. Each day, the Marines purchased at least one block of ice from the icehouse. The empty can was then refilled with potable water and returned to the freezer. When the water buffalo ran low, it was replaced with a full buffalo from the water point. The process became routine, the language barrier diminished, and the mess hall was never without ice to support its operations.

Just before dark on 23 March, MABS-16's TAFDS arrived at Udorn on 1st MAW aircraft. Before noon the following day, a 20,000-gallon system was installed, and civilian contractors filled it with aviation gasoline from tank trucks. On 2 April, a second 20,000-gallon system was installed and filled with JP-4 aviation fuel. These systems were maintained and operated day and night, seven days a week, by one staff sergeant, two corporals, and three lance corporals.

To provide fuel to locations away from the Udorn airfield—which allowed the Air America pilots to refuel their aircraft without having to return to Udorn—the TAFDS Marines began filling 55-gallon drums with aviation gas and having them airlifted to remote sites. Some days, as many as 200 drums were transported to alternate fueling sites. Over time, the Marines accumulated 2,000 such drums to meet their requirement to support the remote fueling sites.

Medical Support

The first flight into the airfield at Udorn on 23 March carried two Navy corpsmen, a field ambulance, and emergency sick-call supplies and equipment. This initial contingent was followed later that day by a medical officer and a third corpsman. By the third day of the deployment, the medical staff had its full complement of eight corpsmen and one medical officer and its medical block, which was capable of supporting 500 men in the field for 30 days. Initially, sick call was conducted out of the field ambulance; by 26 March, however, a general purpose tent had been erected for the medical

staff. Soon thereafter, a dental detachment arrived, and a joint medical/dental sick bay opened for business. Although slightly cramped and dusty, the tent proved adequate, and the combined medical and dental staffs worked successfully there for a month and a half.

By early May, the engineer detachment had rehabilitated the second of the three buildings located in the new cantonment area, and on 8 May the medical officer and his corpsmen moved into their new space at the permanent campsite. It had a roof, was screened in and well lit, and provided sanitary conditions adequate to allow the doctor to perform minor surgery. The plywood deck was also easy to clean and kept insects from entering the sick bay between the floorboards. Further improvements included painting, the installation of white cotton sheeting overhead (which reduced the heat and reflected light), and the installation of a porcelain sink supplied with running water.

The squadron's medical personnel closely monitored field sanitation, a critically important issue in the tropical environment of northeast Thailand. The mess hall was inspected daily. With schistosomiasis—a parasitic disease spread by a waterborne pathogen—a serious problem in northeast Thailand, the medical personnel closely monitored the camp's water supply. Their vigilance meant that water supply problems were not an issue for the entire period of the operation. The heads in the original camp were inspected and the waste incinerated every five to seven days, and in the permanent camp the concrete cistern-chemical heads were treated with unslaked lime twice a week. Insect control, a joint responsibility of the camp police sergeant and sick bay personnel, was managed by use of an applicator that dispensed a DDT fog in the general camp area on a regular schedule.

Sick call was conducted twice daily. In July, a typical month with 253 military personnel on board, 429 outpatient visits were made to the dispensary. Among the medical problems treated were 43 cases of diarrhea and digestive tract infections; 64 diseases of the eyes, ears, nose, and throat; 17 acute respiratory infections; 133 dermatological problems; 2 injuries; 30 surgical conditions; and 8 cases of venereal disease.

Overall, the medical staff encountered few problems during the operation. Some of the more serious medical problems diagnosed and treated during the deployment included 8 cases of malaria, 3 minor fractures, 2 burn cases (1

Pictured here are the message center Marines and technicians who ran and maintained the MABS-16 communications center. The author is third from the right in the front row.

requiring emergency hospitalization), 1 snakebite (that was not life threatening), 2 scorpion stings, 8 cases of heat exhaustion (all in the early weeks of the operation), and 37 cases of venereal disease.

Communications

The communications section was made up of personnel and equipment drawn from the Communications Company, 3d MarDiv, Marine Aircraft Group 16 (MAG-16), and Headquarters & Headquarters Squadron-1, 1st MAW. Its mission was to provide internal communications within the MABS-16 cantonment and to provide voice and encrypted radioteletype communications to the squadron's higher echelons of command located outside of Thailand.

To satisfy the first requirement, MABS-16 deployed with 44 EE-8 battery-powered field telephones, an SB-86 switchboard, and an SB-22 switchboard. Both switchboards were field equipment and, like the phones, were battery operated. Internal communications were quickly established throughout the initial base camp, with additional lines being run as tents were erected and occupied. Concurrent with the construction of the more permanent cantonment, plans were

developed to provide it with telephone service. As soon as the engineers rehabilitated the second of the three existing buildings, the SB-86 switchboard was installed next to the MABS-16 offices, the sick bay, motor transport, and material offices. Lines were quickly run to all offices and work spaces, the flight line, and some of the billeting tents. This system served the squadron's internal communications needs until it departed Thailand in late October.

Prior to passing the telephone exchange to Air America, the Marines made several upgrades to the system. These upgrades included replacing the military "slash wire" connecting each telephone to the main switchboard with WD-110 wire that was more reliable, running all lines overhead, converting to a central battery system, and substituting Air America's desk phones for the Marines' EE-8s.

To satisfy the second element of its mission, the communications section provided links between MABS-16 at Udorn and its supporting organizations on Okinawa and at MCAF Iwakuni,* on the island of Kyushu, Japan. Two major circuits

---

*Naval Air Station Iwakuni was redesignated as Marine Corps Air Facility Iwakuni on 1 January 1958. It was redesignated again as Marine Corps Air Station Iwakuni on 20 July 1962, a designation it still retains today.

Photo courtesy of the author

An AN/TRC-75 transmitter-receiver set up outside of the communications center. The poles in the background support the long-wire antennas that attached to the radio.

were maintained throughout the deployment. The first, which began operations on 23 March, was between Udorn and Bangkok. This circuit employed the AN/TRC-75 transmitter-receiver (state-of-the-art equipment at the time), with supporting TT-4s and AN/GGC-3 teletype machines. The AN/GGC-3 teletype machine employed a paper tape that was perforated each time a key on the keyboard was struck. Complete messages were drafted on these paper tapes. Then, employing a one-time encrypting tape that was duplicated on the receiving end of the circuit, the message was transmitted in encrypted form. The circuit was capable of transmitting voice, Morse code, and teletype signals. The second circuit linked MABS-16 with the Naval Communications Facility in the Philippines (NavComPacPhil). On the Udorn end of this circuit, the Marines employed a CinCPac communications contingency package, provided to MABS-16 specifically to facilitate external communications. Capable of voice and teletype communications, this circuit was established on 8 April and was fully operational by 15 April.

High temperatures, poor signals, and mediocre antennas initially plagued communications on the Bangkok circuit, and teletype incompatibility frustrated communications on the NavComPacPhil circuit. Signals improved markedly on the Bangkok circuit after much experimentation with long-wire antennas cut specifically to frequency length, which were employed at Udorn, and the installation of a 35-foot

fiberglass antenna to the AN/TRC-75 on the Bangkok end of the circuit. The teletype incompatibility problem on the NavComPacPhil circuit was quickly resolved.

Little could be done about the oppressive temperatures and the humidity, but the Marine communicators did take steps to lessen the problems. Early in the deployment, the communications center was moved outside the main camp and into a small wooden garage with a cement floor. This provided a cleaner environment for the communications equipment and allowed fans to be installed, which somewhat cooled the heat-generating communications equipment and delighted the communications center Marines. Two general purpose tents were erected adjacent to the garage where a radio, teletype, switchboard, and telephone maintenance shop was established. As the communications circuits were operational 24 hours a day, a small billeting area was also established in the tents for Marines to use between communications center watches.

During their periods of operation, which ran from 23 March to 26 October, both circuits serviced considerable amounts of traffic. On the Udorn end of the Bangkok circuit, 984 encrypted radioteletype messages were sent, and 2,991 were received. On the Udorn side of the NavComPacPhil net, 1,919 encrypted radioteletype messages were sent and 1,290 were received.

Personnel Programs

The squadron's morale remained high throughout the deployment. It was sustained in part by the knowledge that the Marines were deployed on an actual operational mission. Superb mail service throughout the deployment also contributed to the high morale. The MABS-16 fleet post office address never changed, so mail was delivered regularly. Mail was delivered at least twice weekly on regular courier flights from Futema, Okinawa. Frequently, other flights would stop at Futema and pick up mail waiting to be sent. A post exchange was established on 27 March, less than a week after the Marines began arriving at Udorn. Initially stocked only with necessities, its merchandise expanded considerably when it moved into a larger space in the permanent camp in late April. As the deployment matured and a more normal routine evolved, a volleyball court, horseshoe pits, and two

Marine aircraft, such as this Fairchild R4Q Flying Boxcar, visited the squadron at least twice weekly, carrying mail, repair parts, and other needed supplies.

softball fields were constructed, and an organized athletics program emerged.

In late May, after all of the squadron's personnel had moved to the permanent camp, the Western Pacific Armed Forces Film Exchange began providing the command with five or six movies a week. Free popcorn was provided, and the movies, which were shown in the mess hall, soon became the main source of evening entertainment. Three additional strongback tents erected on a platform served as the special service area. One tent was utilized for beverage sales—both soft drinks and beer could be purchased—and as a lounge area; a second tent housed a ping pong table, a reading area, and a barber shop. The third was equipped with a rostrum for divine services.

After about 10 days, the command initiated a liberty program for the deployed Marines. Liberty was limited to 100 Marines at a time; more than that number, it was determined, would overwhelm the town. As a security measure, Marines of all grades were issued liberty cards and, whenever a Marine was late returning from liberty, the Udorn police turned out every officer on its force to find him.

Travel to and from town—about three miles from the camp—was by *sam lo*, a three-wheeled bicycle-rickshaw peddled by a man in the front with up to two passengers seated in the back. The cost of a one-way trip was three to five Thai *baht*, depending upon the individual Marine's bargaining skills. The exchange rate during the Marines' stay in northeast Thailand remained steady at 20 baht to 1 U.S. dollar. The only bar in town was owned by a Thai army lieutenant who

spoke English and was also the chief of police. It received a considerable amount of business from Marines. Several restaurants were available at which large plates of very spicy beef or chicken fried rice could be purchased for seven baht, and a liter of Thai beer could be had for the same price. The local citizenry was welcoming and friendly, and the Marines reciprocated. There were no adverse incidents for the duration of the deployment.

One- to three-day rest and recreation (R&R) trips to Bangkok began in May. Marines traveled space available on the squadron's R4D-8 or other Marine Corps aircraft. A small bus, operated by the Joint United States Military Assistance Group, brought the vacationing Marines from Don Muang Airport to downtown Bangkok. The centrally located Metropole Hotel, where a double occupancy room with a good bed and air conditioning was available for $5 (100 baht) a day, received most of the R&R business. Meals and drinks were similarly inexpensive. A good steak or lobster dinner at any of the many excellent restaurants cost from $1.50 to $2.00 (30–40 baht). Drinks were about $1 apiece (or 20 baht).

Cab drivers doubled as tour guides and, for a very reasonable price, would take Marines on tours of the city that included stops at several of the many Thai temples. In 1961, the cost of two days in Bangkok was not beyond the reach of even the most junior enlisted Marine, and many took advantage of the opportunity to see one of Southeast Asia's most beautiful and modern cities.

A vibrant and successful people-to-people program received its start from the invitation of a local Udorn

Klongs (canals) run throughout the city of Bangkok. They carry off the monsoon rains and provide a transportation route for farmers to bring their produce from the countryside to sell to city dwellers in floating markets.

basketball team to the Marines to play an exhibition game on the public courts in town. These games soon became nightly affairs featuring several Thai teams and as many as 2,000 people coming to watch. In late summer, the city sponsored a basketball tournament, with several Marine and local Thai teams participating. After several playoff rounds, the MATCU-1 emerged victorious and received a large, engraved silver trophy in recognition of their accomplishment.

In addition to the sports activities, the Marines undertook several projects to assist the local mission church and Catholic school. Through contributions collected at the MABS-16 camp, the Marines purchased materials and a local American contractor laid a concrete floor in the church. Several Marines volunteered to instruct evening English language classes, and several were invited to visit the Udorn Teachers College for Sunday afternoon meetings with the college's English classes.

Aviation Operations

The aircraft maintenance and flight line maintenance Marines quickly adjusted to the rigors of their assignments. While remaining cognizant of their critically important mission to train Air America personnel in aircraft maintenance and flight line operations, they also knew that their immediate goal was to keep the maximum number of Air America aircraft operational. During April—the first full month of operations—they maintained an aircraft availability average

of 18.16 for their 19 HUS-1 helicopters. Flight operations totaled 1,934.5 flight hours, for an average of 106.5 hours of flying time per helicopter. In May, the average aircraft availability was 18.6 with a total of 1,750 flight hours.

The high availability rates were not achieved without much hard work on the part of the crews and included many major repairs and the replacement of major aircraft components. During these initial two months of operation, the maintenance crews conducted 24 periodic calendar inspections, 19 engine build-ups/replacements, 5 main transmission changes, 8 major rotor changes, and 76 other component changes. They also repaired structural damage caused by 73 bullet strikes. The avionics shop serviced 115 major end items of helicopter equipment. With operational requirements demanding the maximum availability of aircraft, work was extended into the evenings, particularly on the flight line where the Marines made concerted efforts to correct all aircraft discrepancies before morning.

While June saw a significant decrease in battle damage, it was becoming increasingly more costly in maintenance hours and effort to keep the overworked aircraft in the air. The

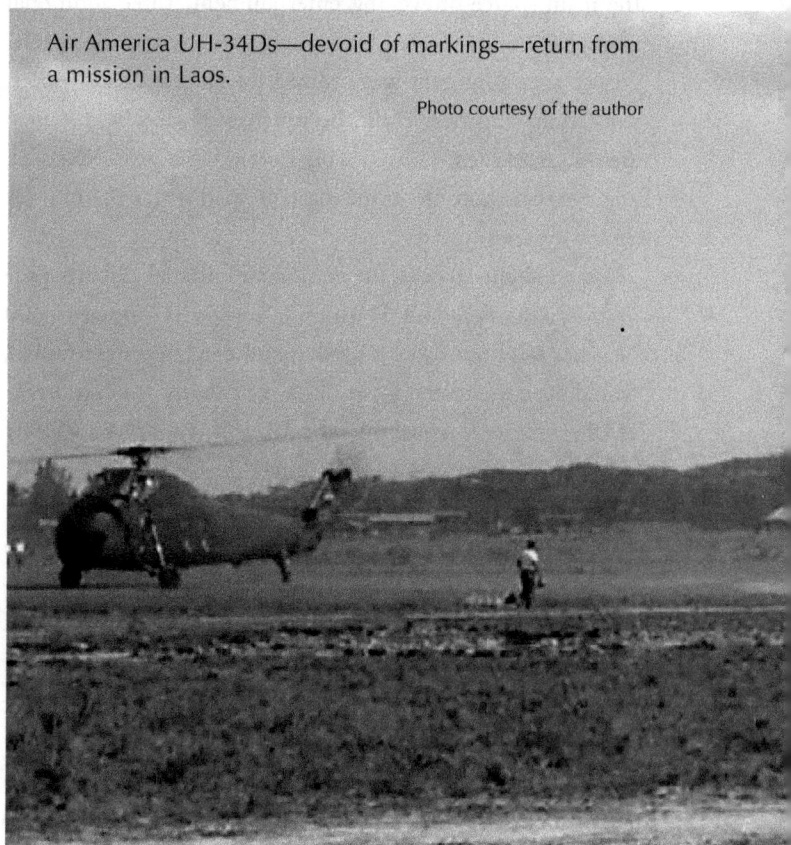

Air America UH-34Ds—devoid of markings—return from a mission in Laos.

maintenance issues were exacerbated by frequent shortages of critical spare parts. During June, for example, 60 aircraft-days were lost while awaiting spare parts. There was a solution to this problem, but it was not without cost. The number of aircraft grounded as a result of the lack of spare parts could be appreciably reduced by switching parts between aircraft. However, this practice added significantly to the maintenance workload measured in the increased hours required to take parts off one aircraft and install them on another to make it flightworthy. Nevertheless, in June eight tail rotor assemblies, two main rotors, two engine packages, and numerous other items (such as carburetors, inverters, and instruments) were exchanged between aircraft. The Marines simply worked the extra hours to keep more aircraft in the air.

Air America resupply stock levels at Don Muang Airport in Bangkok, the source of the maintenance department's spare parts, were inadequate to meet the requirements of 20 helicopters flying excessively long hours. Further, its spare parts records cards contained a mix of Navy and Air Force parts identifying numbers, which caused confusion when Air America entered the Navy supply system at the Naval Supply Depot in Yokosuka, Japan, to order replacement parts. To solve this problem, the noncommissioned officer in charge of the Navy supply section located with the aircraft maintenance department at Udorn traveled to Don Muang Airport to establish a workable system that forwarded all spare part requisitions to the Naval Supply Depot in the Navy's "language." This sped up the resupply process and raised Air America's stock levels at Don Muang. While the level of spare parts improved, the maintenance crews at Udorn continued to be plagued by shortages for the duration of their tours.

Aircraft losses further reduced operational readiness. On 16 June, an HUS-1 made a forced landing on a sandbar in the Mekong River. Several days of troubleshooting, during which a number of engine accessories were replaced, failed to return the aircraft to operational condition. To bring the helicopter to a location where more extensive repairs could be made required pulling it through water that reached the level of its cockpit. Once this was accomplished, the malfunctioning engine was replaced, but it was 30 June before it was returned to Udorn and put back into service. On 18 June, another HUS-1 was seriously damaged after aborting

a landing from an altitude of 4,300 feet. Unable to slow his rate of descent, the pilot settled his helicopter on a steep slope near the landing site. The helicopter rolled over twice before coming to a stop. Although selected items were salvaged, the aircraft was beyond repair and destroyed.

There was significantly less work in July for the maintenance department's Marines as a result of a month of no battle damage and a sharply reduced requirement to perform major component changes. Despite this reduced workload, the maintenance crews kept an average of 16.9 aircraft in the air for a total of 1,625 flying hours, or an average of 96 hours per aircraft. One aircraft was lost due to an engine malfunction when the pilot was forced to land at an inaccessible site and the aircraft could not be recovered. On 23 and 24 July, two C-124s brought two HUS-1s to Udorn as replacements for the lost aircraft. They were quickly assembled and given the requisite test flights. No discrepancies were found, so they were immediately placed in operation.

From MABS-16's arrival at the Udorn airfield in late March, Air America personnel had worked closely with the aircraft maintenance and flight line Marines to acquire the knowledge they needed to completely run operations when the Marines departed. With the end of July near, the 120-day mark—the outside limit of the Marines' expected stay—was approaching. As a first positive step toward the MABS-16 phase-out, Air America assumed responsibility for all flight line functions on 23 July. Marines retained refueling responsibilities and continued to operate the TAFDS, and a senior staff noncommissioned officer remained on the flight line as an advisor and coordinator between flight line and hangar maintenance crews.

August proved to be a busy month for the maintenance department. In response to a Thai request, two Marine HUS-1s were deployed within Thailand to relocate the relay stations of a Thai TRC-24 radio relay system. Tragedy struck on 15 August when one of the helicopters burned after crashing in dense jungle just short of its designated landing site. The crash killed two passengers, and three crew members were seriously injured as a result of burns. The crew chief also sustained a compound fracture of his lower left leg. On 28 August, the second helicopter experienced engine failure and was forced down approximately 150 miles from the Marine base at Udorn. An engine package, borrowed from

Air America, was trucked to the site of the downed aircraft and installed by Marines, who were assisted by members of the Royal Thai Air Force. The helicopter returned to Udorn on 2 September.

Concurrently, Marines and Air America maintenance crews remained busy supporting operations taking place in Laos. During August, with an average of 15.3 helicopters available, Air America crews flew a total of 1,569 hours for an average of 102.5 hours per aircraft. A serious in-flight accident that resulted in extensive fuselage damage on the port side of an HUS-1 required a major repair effort. To return the aircraft to full flight status required the replacement of 8 square feet of external skin and several supporting ribs in the area around the left pylon and an additional 14 square feet of skin and several supporting ribs on the outside of the radio compartment. Availability of spare parts continued to plague the maintenance crews. Thirty-six aircraft days were lost in the month because the parts to put aircraft back into service could not be found.

On 8 August, an Air America helicopter was shot down behind enemy lines. After making an emergency landing, the crew escaped and spent three days evading enemy forces. All of the crew members were rescued with only minor injuries. The four helicopters involved in the search-and-rescue effort required significant repairs for damage resulting from enemy small-arms fire.

While the Marines continued to perform most of the maintenance functions, the plan to transfer responsibility for all maintenance activities to Air America remained on track. In August, 27 experienced Air America general aircraft mechanics arrived. They were assigned full time to classroom instruction during the day to familiarize them with the HUS-1. They were then assigned an evening shift on the flight line. Earlier in the month, a Sikorsky factory representative had arrived to provide technical assistance during the transition. He served primarily as a classroom instructor for the new Air America employees. Late in the month, a tentative agreement was reached with the Air America station manager to effect the complete transfer of aircraft maintenance responsibilities in late September, or well into the sixth month of the deployment.

Between 1 and 22 September, 15 helicopters were available for flight operations, on average, and a total of 856.1

hours were flown. Battle damage increased somewhat during this period, with repairs required on seven aircraft. On 4 September, an HUS-1 was extensively damaged making a landing in rough terrain. After being hit by enemy fire while attempting to land in the primary zone, the pilot diverted to a secondary site where his aircraft sustained major fuselage damage when it struck a hidden tree stump. On 9 September, small-arms fire damaged a helicopter's tail rotor, necessitating the removal and replacement of the complete tail rotor assembly.

The schedule for passing responsibility for aircraft maintenance from the Marines to Air America accelerated in September. On 5 September, Air America assumed responsibility for the tool room. Supplies not needed by Air America's maintenance crews were made ready for shipment back to MAG-16 on Okinawa. The following day, 10 additional Air America mechanics arrived. They immediately began a six-day instruction period on the HUS-1 led by the Sikorsky technical representative. With Air America personnel now assuming much of the maintenance workload, Marines began preparing in earnest for their departure. On 8 September, six enlisted Marines detached and returned to MAG-16. The following day, the squadron's maintenance officer was detached.

On 20 September, an Air America representative assumed responsibility for all maintenance equipment and supplies that were to be left behind. All other equipment and supplies were inventoried and boxed for return to MAG-16. At 1630 on 22 September, with a total of 54 personnel assigned to the maintenance department, Air America assumed all responsibility for aircraft maintenance. In the avionics shop, where staffing was still inadequate to sustain operations, three Marines remained to assist and instruct. By the beginning of October, 6 additional civilian avionics employees had arrived, bringing the total civilian strength to 12 and matching the number of Marines that had staffed the avionics shop. With operations now running satisfactorily and with only infrequent assistance required, the Marine avionics personnel were phased out and returned to Okinawa on 15 October 1961.

The aircraft maintenance section's Marines were not the only ones planning for departure from Udorn. By early September, a plan had been finalized for the complete relief of MABS-16 and the assumption of duties by Air America. The plan was executed, with departures beginning in September

and accelerating in October. Functions required to maintain operational capability were staffed with the minimum number of Marines until the very end. Those assigned to the aviation maintenance section, as noted previously, remained until the middle of October. Communications circuits remained open, and responsibility for the camp's internal phone system was not passed to Air America until late October. Other Marines remained, as required, until the remaining Marines departed Udorn on 26 October 1961.

It would not be long, however, before Marines in greater numbers returned to Thailand. In early 1962, increased fighting broke out in Laos, with the very real threat that hostilities would spill across the border into Thailand. To ensure the territorial integrity of Thailand and to block the spread of Communism in Southeast Asia, the Corps returned to Thailand in Marine expeditionary unit strength.

Shufly: April 1962–January 1963

The Communist offensive in South Vietnam continued to expand in the early 1960s, and to address this threat the South Vietnamese government increased the size of its armed forces. Deficiencies in the ARVN's and the VNMC's capabilities were many; however, among the most serious was their lack of mobility. The United States stepped in to fill this void, and by early 1962, three U.S. Army helicopter companies were providing combat support to South Vietnam's forces.

A CinCPac assessment of support requirements conducted in early 1962 identified the need for a fourth Army light helicopter company to support RVN operations in the Mekong Delta region. The assessment recommended that an additional U.S. Army helicopter company be deployed to support the RVN forces. On 6 March 1962, the secretary of defense approved this recommendation, and the Joint Chiefs of Staff (JCS) directed the Army to provide the unit.

Two days before Admiral Felt forwarded his recommendation to the secretary of defense, General Timmes, the MAAG chief, had recommended that nine Marine helicopter pilots receive temporary 60- to 90-day assignments to Army helicopter units to familiarize them with helicopter combat support operations in South Vietnam. When Admiral Felt passed this recommendation to General Shapley, commanding general of FMFPac, the general demurred, citing several reasons why the assignments would not benefit either the

Army or the Marines. In a counterproposal, General Shapley recommended that a complete Marine medium helicopter squadron be deployed instead and that it replace the Army helicopter company in Da Nang. This would assign a Marine helicopter squadron to South Vietnam's northernmost tactical zone (I Corps)—where the Marines believed they would be assigned if they were sent to South Vietnam in organized combat units. Further, it would free the Army company to deploy to the Mekong Delta area and support ARVN operations there in concert with the other currently assigned Army helicopter companies.

Admiral Felt forwarded this proposal to the affected commands for their comments. General Harkins, commander USMACV, concurred but proposed that the Marine helicopter squadron initially be assigned to Soc Trang in the Mekong Delta. In his view, the Marine squadron could trade places with the Army helicopter company at Da Nang at a future date. Admiral Felt and General Harkins jointly forwarded this recommendation to the JCS, who approved it on 16 March 1962. Admiral Felt immediately ordered a Marine helicopter squadron be deployed to South Vietnam, with an arrival date of 15 April.

On 22 March, Major General John P. Condon, commanding general, 1st MAW, was directed to designate a Marine medium helicopter squadron from his command for duty in South Vietnam. At the time, General Condon was at his field headquarters on the Philippine island of Mindoro, where he was participating in Operation Tulungen, a major SEATO training exercise. The unit to be assigned—Marine Medium Helicopter Squadron 362 (HMM-362)—was also deployed on Operation Tulungen as were most of the senior 1st MAW staff officers who would develop the plans and recommend the size and structure of the unit to be deployed. The deployment was given the code name "Shufly." Operation Tulungan was scheduled to run for approximately one more week, which would give HMM-362 just two weeks to make the 15 April scheduled arrival time in South Vietnam.

General Condon took full advantage of the operation's remaining few days, including the fact that he had all of his senior planners and the designated squadron at hand. As noted by Lieutenant Colonel Archie J. Clapp, the commanding officer of HMM-362, "Planning was accomplished at his [Condon's] command post on Mindoro, where all essential details were nailed down in a few days, with no appreciable disruption to Tulungen."

Deployment

Shufly was activated on 4 April 1962, only 11 days before the scheduled arrival of HMM-362 in South Vietnam. Prior to its activation, General Condon had proposed command relationships and a command structure that organized the Marine aviation unit into three separate elements. The entire organization would be under the operational command of USMACV's commander, with the commanding general of 1st MAW retaining administrative control. Designated Task Unit 79.3.5, the headquarters (Task Element [TE] 79.3.5.0) comprised a task unit commander plus seven other officers and six enlisted Marines. The first commander of the task unit, Colonel John F. Carey, was a Marine aviator who had earned the Navy Cross for heroism during the Battle of Midway.

The second element of the task unit was the helicopter squadron, HMM-362 (Reinforced) (TE 79.3.5.1), under the command of Colonel Clapp. Clapp had enlisted in the Marine Corps in 1940 and been commissioned in 1943. As an aviator, he had distinguished himself in the final months of World War II and during the Korean War.

In addition to its normal complement of 63 officers and 196 enlisted Marines, HMM-362 was augmented with 50 additional maintenance personnel. Its complement of aircraft included 24 Sikorsky UH-34D helicopters, which could carry between 11 and 12 combat-loaded troops when flying under normal conditions and close to sea level. (In 1962, the HUS-1 Seahorse was redesignated as the UH-34 Seahorse.) In addition, the squadron was assigned three Cessna OE-1 Bird Dogs—a single-engine observation aircraft—and one Douglas R4D transport for personnel, supplies, and equipment.

The third element was a subunit of MABS-16 (TE 79.3.5.2), commanded by Lieutenant Colonel William W. Eldridge. Included with the subunit's 18 officers and 193 enlisted Marines were a Navy chaplain and Navy medical and dental personnel. It was further augmented with a TAFDS and a Marine airfield traffic control unit. Organic to the control unit were tactical air navigation and ground control approach systems. These systems enabled the squadron's helicopters to make landings during periods of reduced visibility.

Lieutenant Colonel Archie J. Clapp

Official U.S. Marine Corps photo

Lieutenant Colonel Archie J. Clapp commanded the first Marine Corps tactical unit— HMM-362—to serve in combat in the Vietnam War.

Born in Glenwood, North Carolina, on 30 August 1921, Clapp spent his childhood years in Miami, Florida, where he attended grammar and high school. He later earned a bachelor of science degree at the University of Maryland. He enlisted in the Marine Corps in 1940 and, following boot camp, was assigned to an aviation billet at Quantico, Virginia.

Clapp attended flight training at Pensacola, Florida, as an enlisted Marine. Upon graduation in July 1943,

he was designated a naval aviator and commissioned a second lieutenant. He received operational flight training at Naval Air Station Jacksonville, Florida, before assignment to Marine Fighter Squadron 123 at Santa Barbara, California. In early 1945 he was transferred to the Pacific Theater.

While in the Pacific, Clapp served as an F4U Corsair pilot on board the USS *Bennington* (CV 20) and flew in the Iwo Jima and Okinawa campaigns. He was among the first carrier-based pilots to fly combat missions against the Japanese homeland. During his tour, he was credited with shooting down three enemy aircraft. Ordered home at the conclusion of the war, Clapp served in several stateside squadrons and attended various military schools. In March 1951, he joined Marine Experimental Squadron 1 at Quantico where he became proficient in helicopters.

Ordered to Korea in November 1952, Clapp split his tour, initially flying helicopters with Marine Transport Helicopter Squadron 161 and then flying as an attack pilot with Marine Composite Squadron 1. In June 1953 he was assigned as the commanding officer, Headquarters Squadron 37, 3d Marine Aircraft Wing, Miami, Florida. A tour as the helicopter operations officer at

the Marine Corps Development Center, Quantico, followed. From 1956 to 1959, Clapp served at Headquarters Marine Corps as the assistant secretary of the General Staff.

His headquarters tour was followed by assignment to MCAS, Santa Ana, California. While there, he was advanced to lieutenant colonel and assumed command of HMM-362. He deployed the squadron in July 1961, first to Okinawa and then to the USS *Princeton* (LPH 5) as the air element of the Seventh Fleet's amphibious ready group. In April 1962, he again deployed the squadron, this time to Soc Trang, South Vietnam, to command the first Marine Corps tactical unit to serve in combat against Viet Cong and North Vietnamese forces.

Upon returning to the United States, Colonel Clapp was assigned as the executive officer of the Marine Air Reserve Training Detachment, Naval Air Station Minneapolis, Minnesota. Attendance at the Army War College followed. In July 1965, he was assigned as the assistant head of the Military Personnel Procurement Branch at Headquarters Marine Corps. The following year, Clapp was assigned to the Joint Staff where he served as a member of the J-5 (Strategic Plans and Policy Directorate) until he retired.

From his headquarters at MCAF Iwakuni, Japan, Colonel Carey and his task group staff coordinated planning for the deployment with subordinate units that were located at Naval Air Station Atsugi, Japan, several hundred miles to the north, and at MCAF Futema, Okinawa, over a thousand miles to the south. In coordination with Marine Aerial Refueler Transport Squadron 152 (VMGR-152), Colonel Carey's staff quickly worked out the details of the airlift for the MABS-16 subunit and his task unit headquarters. The Navy carrier task unit, also activated on 4 April, included the amphibious assault ship (helicopter carrier) USS *Princeton* (LPH 5) and escort destroyers. It had the responsibility for transporting the HMM-362 helicopters to the waters off the coast of South Vietnam.

The airlift portion of the movement began on 9 April. The destination for Colonel Carey's task unit was an old, 3,000-foot Japanese-built runway near the small town of Soc Trang in Ba Xuyen Province. Just 20 miles from the coast and 85 miles southwest of Saigon, the airstrip was one of the few hard-surface runways in the southern region. The Marine helicopters would operate from this location until they were ordered north to Da Nang. At 0800 on 9 April 1962, Colonel Carey and some of his staff landed at Soc Trang on board an R4D. General Condon, the 1st MAW commander, flew the first Lockheed GV-1 Hercules tanker (redesignated as KC-130 in 1962) into Soc Trang. General Hawkins and Brigadier General Le Van Nghiem, the Vietnamese III Corps commander, were there to greet Colonel Carey and the Marines.

Colonel Eldridge's MABS-16 subunit Marines, who had also been flown in, began readying the airfield for the squadron's arrival, only six days away. Seventy-five strong-back tents, all with plywood decks, were raised, and a water purification unit was set up. A field laundry and mess hall were established, and by 12 April the Marines were enjoying hot meals. The post office became operational and telephones were installed, connecting the billeting and working areas. An old Japanese hangar was rehabilitated to house some of the squadron's aircraft and equipment. The communications section became operational with USMACV in Saigon and MAG-16 on Okinawa. The TAFDS was assembled and filled with aviation fuel and MATCU-68 was prepared to conduct flight operations.

While HMM-362 was participating in Operation Tulungan, Colonel Clapp was informed that his squadron would be ordered to South Vietnam in support of Shufly. Because the planned deployment was classified, he could not immediately share the information with the members of his squadron. When Operation Tulungan ended on 1 April 1962, only two weeks remained before HMM-362 was required to arrive at Soc Trang. The squadron loaded on board the *Princeton* for its return to Okinawa. To provide the squadron with aircraft that had the greatest operating times before required overhauls, the *Princeton* stopped briefly at Subic Bay in the Philippines to exchange some of HMM-362's aircraft for a like number of helicopters from its sister squadron. With that accomplished, the *Princeton* steamed to Okinawa to pick up the remainder of the squadron's personnel and equipment.

On 10 April, with HMM-362 and its reinforcements aboard, the *Princeton* departed Buckner Bay, Okinawa, for the coast of South Vietnam. The task group (the *Princeton* was one ship in Amphibious Ready Group Task Group 76.5) arrived early on the morning of 15 April, and Colonel Clapp led the first flight of helicopters to the airfield at Soc Trang. The operation went smoothly, and by midafternoon the airlift of all of HMM-362's helicopters, personnel, and equipment had been completed. Helicopters from HMM-261 that had assisted in the lift returned to the *Princeton* to continue duties as the helicopter element of the amphibious ready group. On 16 April 1962, HMM-362, nicknamed "Archie's Angels," was prepared to support ARVN and VNMC operations in South Vietnam's III Corps.

The deployment of a Marine helicopter squadron to South Vietnam garnered a considerable amount of attention from the U.S. press, which took the occasion not only to report on the addition of U.S. military support to South Vietnam, but also to speculate on its long-term implications. Some reporting accurately portrayed events, while other accounts were wide of the mark. In the latter case, the *Washington Post* reported on 15 April that "the first U.S. Marine Corps advisors will arrive in South Viet-Nam Sunday under a U.S. aid program, an American military spokesman said today." In fact, HMM-362 had not deployed to South Vietnam in an advisory role. Furthermore, Marines had been serving in advisory capacities in South Vietnam since February 1955. In a more accurate identification of the Marine squadron's

U.S. Marine officers gather around the village priest in the fortified village of Rach Trang in the the River Bassac Fleuve estuary. From left: LtCol Robert L. Rathbun, commanding officer of HMM-163; Father Phuoc; LtCol Archie J. Clapp, commanding officer of HMM-362; Col Julius W. Ireland, commander Task Force 79.3.5; MajGen Richard G. Weede, chief of staff, USMACV; and French interpreter Gilles H. Rocheleau. General Weede presented the village with a bull on 24 July 1962.

role, the *New York Times* reported in articles on 16 and 17 April 1962 that a Marine helicopter unit had arrived in South Vietnam and would be located near the Ba Xuyen provincial capital of Soc Trang, approximately 100 miles southwest of Saigon. Also correctly noted was the unit's primary mission: "to airlift Vietnamese combat troops into areas occupied by Vietcong guerrillas." In a broader assessment offered five days later, a *New York Times* reporter stated that the U.S. role in South Vietnam had "become of decisive importance" and that "the United States has shouldered a sweeping commitment, the future scope, hazards and duration of which are highly uncertain." It concluded, presciently, by noting that the United States alone would not be able to dictate the final outcome of the conflict: "The main burden of the conflict must fall on the South Vietnamese; if they slacken and divide, if the Ngo Dinh Diem regime proves unable to maintain unity and morale, the best United States efforts could prove unavailing."

Combat Operations

In the days immediately following its arrival, the squadron received no missions. The pilots therefore began flying to familiarize themselves with their new surroundings. They

discovered that their area of operations was very large, stretching from north and east of Saigon to the southernmost tip of the country, the Ca Mau Peninsula. On the east, it was bordered by the South China Sea and on the west by Cambodia. The countryside was laced with thousands of canals and trails, and numerous hamlets—most enclosed by hedgerows or tree lines—dotted the landscape. Characteristic of the dry season, the rice paddies were dusty, brown, and dry; the monsoon rains would change that in the months ahead. Along the coast and flanking the larger rivers, the pilots saw verdant mangrove swamps. They also flew over III Corps' major towns: Soc Trang, My Tho, and Can Tho. These towns, the pilots learned, were under the control of the national government; the loyalties of the villages and hamlets were often in doubt.

HMM-362's first combat mission came on Easter Sunday, 22 April 1962, when it supported the U.S. Army's 57th Helicopter Company in a movement of elements of the ARVN's 7th Division. After flying the 50-plus miles northeast from Soc Trang to My Tho, the pilots flew a total of 29 sorties, lifting 400 Vietnamese soldiers without incident. Later that same day, the squadron was called upon to evacuate an American advisor from Vinh Long, an outpost located some 46

III Corps Tactical Zone 1962

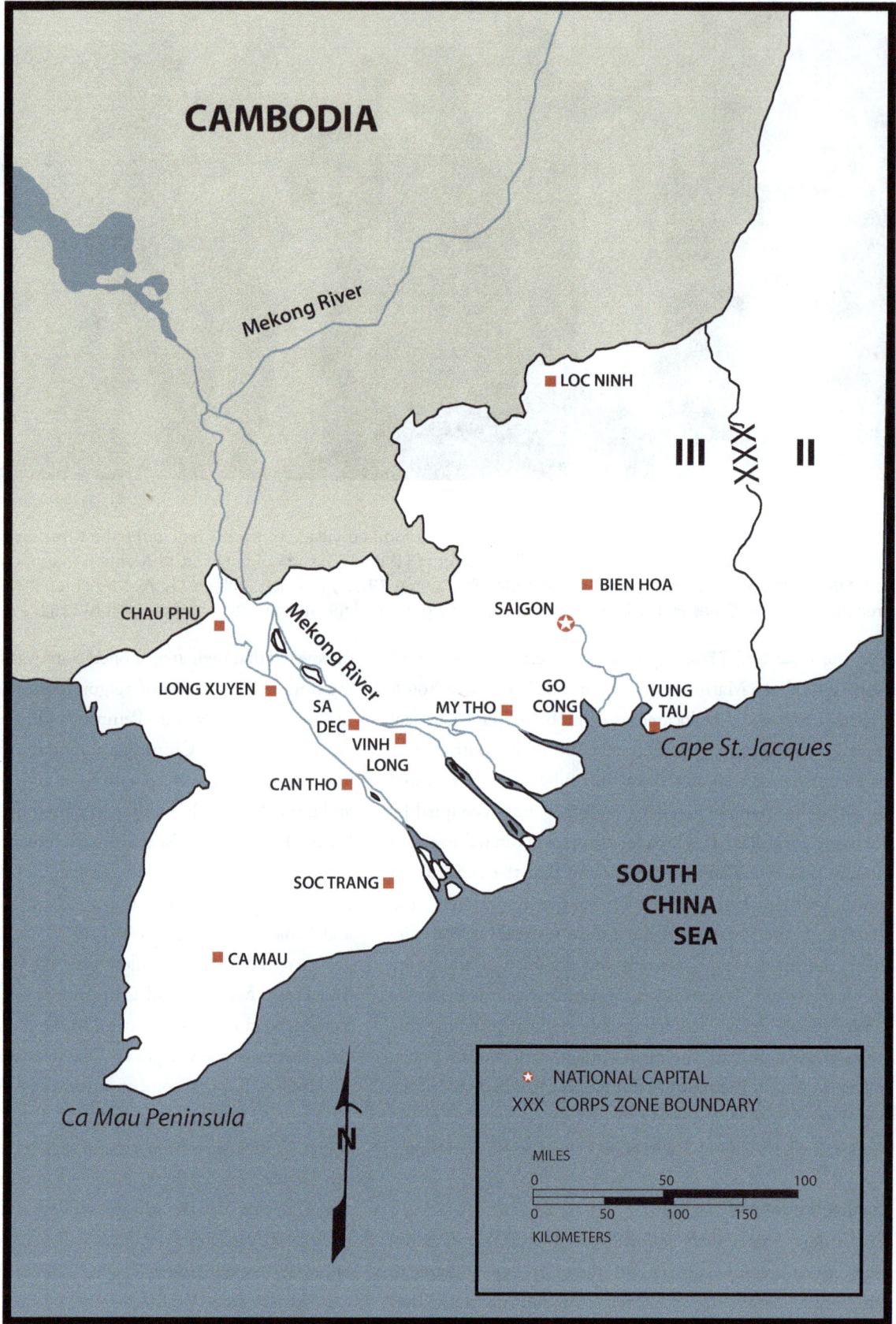

CAMBODIA

Mekong River

LOC NINH

III XXX II

BIEN HOA

SAIGON ☆

CHAU PHU

Mekong River

LONG XUYEN

SA DEC

VINH LONG

MY THO

GO CONG

VUNG TAU

Cape St. Jacques

CAN THO

SOUTH CHINA SEA

SOC TRANG

CA MAU

Ca Mau Peninsula

N

☆ NATIONAL CAPITAL

XXX CORPS ZONE BOUNDARY

MILES

0   50   100

0   50   100   150

KILOMETERS

miles north of Soc Trang. On 23 April, HMM-362 conducted its first operation in support of the Vietnamese marines. The squadron airlifted a VNMC company into a threatened government outpost south of the town of Ca Mau, near the southern tip of the country. While the Vietnamese marines provided security, HMM-362 evacuated the 57-man garrison.

The squadron was in action again on 24 April and suffered its first combat damage. Flying in support of Operation Nightingale near the town of Can Tho, HMM-362 lifted 591 troops of the 21st ARVN Division into eight landing zones along two canals where a large concentration of Viet Cong had been spotted. In the intense firefight that ensued, one helicopter was forced to land after enemy small-arms fire punctured an oil line. The crew was quickly recovered, and ARVN forces surrounded the downed aircraft. A repair crew was flown in, and the downed helicopter was repaired in two hours. Overall, the operation was deemed a success. The Viet Cong lost a reported 70 killed and 3 captured. The ARVN division reported that three of its members had been killed and six were wounded.

The operational tempo increased and with it the experience levels of the pilots and their crew chiefs. Lessons learned were quickly incorporated into the squadron's tactics to improve operational efficiency and lessen the danger to the pilots and crews, their aircraft, and their passengers. One operational hazard the aircrews became acquainted with early in their tours was first encountered while landing in unpredictable terrain. After landing and shutting down an aircraft on what appeared to be hard, dry ground, the pilots soon noticed that the aircraft's landing gear was slowly sinking into the ground. Lumber was quickly placed under the helicopter's axles, and while the aircraft continued to sink into the earth, the engine was started. The pilots engaged the rotors and were successful in lifting the aircraft into the air. After this incident, the squadron's helicopters always carried short lengths of Marston matting for the crew chiefs to insert under the wheels before the aircraft were shut down.

Loading South Vietnamese soldiers in the early weeks of the squadron's deployment revealed another problem. Their short stature made it difficult for them to get into the helicopter's cabin from solid ground and impossible if they were standing in mud. Innovative squadron metalsmiths resolved this problem by constructing steps that could be attached to the helicopter cabin's entryway.

Load capacities were also of critical importance to the squadron and its pilots. Once established, they varied little

Sikorsky UH-34Ds of HMM-362, led by LtCol Archie J. Clapp, transport ARVN soldiers in operations against Viet Cong insurgents in the Mekong Delta in May 1962.

Photo courtesy of LtCol James P. Kizer

during the initial months of operations. Under normal conditions in the Mekong Delta, which was close to sea level, the UH-34D could carry approximately 1,700 pounds in addition to its two pilots and crew chief. Estimating the weight of the individual Vietnamese soldier at 150 pounds—55 pounds less than the estimate for an American soldier—the UH-34D could typically transport 11–12 ARVN or VNMC troops between the pick up and landing zones. This estimation assumed the full fuel load that was normally carried on initial lifts.

An important and potentially life saving lesson was learned on 9 May when the squadron supported ARVN troops in a helicopter assault on the Viet Cong–controlled village of Cai Ngai, 21 miles south of Ca Mau. Immediately following Vietnamese Air Force (VNAF) preparatory strikes, 22 of HMM-362's helicopters split into six smaller flights and began their approach to the six intended landing zones. Firing broke out before the ARVN soldiers could exit the Marine helicopters, resulting in small-arms hits on eight aircraft. One South Vietnamese soldier was killed and another wounded while still inside the aircraft. One aircraft was forced to land a short distance from Cai Ngai. It was quickly surrounded by friendly forces, repaired, and returned to Soc Trang. From this operation, the Marine pilots learned that in the heavily populated delta area the Viet Cong could, if forewarned by fixed-wing aircraft preparatory air strikes, very quickly converge on suspected landing zones to oppose arriving forces. As the element of surprise was compromised by these strikes, the Marines decided to forgo them in future operations in the flat delta region.

As the deployment progressed, HMM-362's missions increased both in number and in variety. On 23 May, two UH-34Ds performed a night medical evacuation that earned the squadron the personal thanks of the 7th ARVN Division commander. At 2000, when the evacuation request was received, the pilots faced a ragged 300-foot ceiling with visibility limited by rainfall. Flying from Soc Trang and navigating by dead reckoning, the helicopters found the pickup site some 30 miles southwest of Saigon. Guided by a bonfire, the Marine helicopters landed in the landing zone and took on board two South Vietnamese officers who were suffering from severe head wounds. A short while later, the wounded officers were delivered to a Saigon hospital. The 7th ARVN

Division commander said that the HMM-362 pilots had performed the first-ever night helicopter evacuation and that the effect of the "med-evac" on the morale and fighting spirit of his men was immeasurable.

In response to an increasingly elusive enemy that all too frequently was able to successfully flee from attacking ARVN soldiers, Colonels Carey and Clapp devised a tactic to prevent these escapes from occurring. Code-named "Eagle Flight," the plan called for four additional helicopters, each carrying 12 ARVN soldiers, to circle adjacent to the operational area. When Viet Cong were observed fleeing the area, the South Vietnamese soldiers in the Eagle Flight helicopters would be landed in a position to block their escape. The concept was first tested on 18 June when HMM-362 flew ARVN forces into 16 separate landing sites. While monsoon rains made finding the enemy difficult, Marine pilots sighted approximately 10 Viet Cong in an area adjacent to the main landing site. Eagle Flight forces were called in, and the ARVN soldiers captured 10 enemy combatants and wounded another. A few days later, an Eagle Flight made two successful forays against the enemy.

In the first, Marine helicopters landed ARVN soldiers who, in short order, killed four Viet Cong and captured a fifth. Reboarding the helicopters, the ARVN soldiers were quickly ferried to a second site where they took an additional four enemy soldiers prisoner. On 10 July, after landing 968 ARVN soldiers into the Ca Mau area, HMM-362 had three opportunities to employ Eagle Flight. While the operation was underway, Eagle Flight crews observed a sampan (a flat-bottomed wooden boat) moving to the north and away from the operating area. They quickly placed ARVN troops ahead of the sampan and intercepted it. Later in the day, the flight clashed twice with a force that was estimated to be a Viet Cong platoon. Although all four Marine helicopters were hit by small-arms fire during these engagements, the first resulted in seven enemy killed and several weapons captured, and the second resulted in six additional enemy dead and more weapons captured. The Marines were learning, and their willingness to innovate and experiment was bringing increased successes to their operations.

In another new dimension to the counterguerrilla capabilities of the Marine helicopter squadron, HMM-362 conducted its first night helicopter assault on 20 July. Launching from Soc Trang at 0415, 16 UH-34Ds lifted 494 ARVN soldiers in three waves and landed them in zones on the Plain of Reeds about 40 miles southwest of the town of Ben Tre. The operations plan called for the ARVN soldiers to encircle a suspected Viet Cong village before dawn and then attack it at daybreak. HMM-362 completed its part of the mission without incident 10 minutes before daylight. Although it was a very difficult mission to accomplish, Colonel Clapp attributed his squadron's success, in part, to the nearly perfect flying conditions. The moonlight reflecting from the flat, flooded rice paddies aided the Marine pilots in their advance to the objective and in identifying their landing zones.

As the squadron continued to execute a full schedule of missions throughout the month of July, the time for its relief was drawing near. Major General Carson A. Roberts's staff at FMFPac had developed a policy, approved by the CMC, that called for the replacement of the in-country squadron after a period of approximately four months by a like squadron from the 3d MAW in California. Similarly, Marines serving with the task unit headquarters and with the MABS-16 subunit were to be replaced by MAG-16 Marines from Futema, Okinawa.

The lead elements of HMM-163, commanded by Lieutenant Colonel Robert L. Rathbun, a veteran fighter pilot from WWII and Korea, began arriving at Soc Trang on 23 July. Airlifted by Marine Hercules aircraft from MCAF Santa Ana, California, they were soon followed by the remainder of the squadron. HMM-163 brought neither helicopters nor maintenance equipment. As had been previously decided, the squadron simply "fell in" on the aircraft and maintenance facilities being employed by HMM-362. During their last week of operations, HMM-362's veteran crews flew with the HMM-163 pilots to orient them to the operational environment. These orientation flights included participation in two operational missions. On 27 July, an 18-aircraft mission flew an ARVN combat unit to an area about 20 miles northeast of Soc Trang, and on 28 July, 21 HMM-362 helicopters supported a 21st ARVN Division operation near Ca Mau. During the latter airlift, Eagle Flight was committed four times. HMM-163 officially relieved HMM-362 on 1 August 1962.

In 107 days of combat support operations, HMM-362 had compiled an impressive record. Significantly, the squadron had suffered no combat casualties and, although 17 of its 24 helicopters and 2 of its 3 OE-1 Bird Dogs sustained battle damage, no aircraft had been lost. Archie's Angels had executed 50 combat helicopter assaults, flown 4,439 sorties, and logged 5,262 hours of combat flight time.

HMM-362's departure closely coincided with the departure of some of the senior Marine officers who had served during the genesis of Shufly. On 30 July, Colonel Carey was relieved as the commander of Task Unit 79.3.5 by Colonel Julius W. Ireland, another Marine aviator who had seen service in two wars. He had also previously served in Vietnam. In April 1954, as commander of Marine Attack Squadron 324 (VMA-324), he had flown into Da Nang to deliver 25 Vought F4U/FG Corsair fighter-bombers to the French who badly needed them to support their forces at Dien Bien Phu. Lastly, on 4 August 1962, the MABS-16 subunit changed hands when Colonel Eldridge was relieved by Lieutenant Colonel Ralph R. Davis. The first chapter of Marine helicopter operations in South Vietnam—so well written by this original cast—had come to a close.

HMM-163—known as "Rathbun's Ridge Runners"—lost no time going into action. On 1 August, the day the squadron assumed responsibility for flight operations, it joined the Army's 57th Helicopter Company in a coordinated troop lift. A few days later, the squadron participated in a 2,000-man movement in An Xuyen—South Vietnam's southernmost province. This started a week-long operation against a Viet Cong stronghold in which the squadron conducted several additional lifts and resulted in the ARVN reporting 84 Communists killed and 30 captured, as well as the confiscation of nearly 15,000 pounds of weapons, ammunition, and explosives. The operation also resulted in the loss of the first Marine UH-34D when a VNAF fighter careened off the runway at Soc Trang and crashed into the helicopter, damaging it beyond repair.

In August, the squadron's aircraft sustained their first combat damage. On 18 August, a 14-aircraft flight led by Colonel Rathbun arrived at a landing site to pick up a group of ARVN soldiers, but there were no ARVN soldiers in the zone. A pilot reported seeing a group of ARVN soldiers at a site approximately half a mile away, and when a white smoke signal appeared in that area, Colonel Rathbun diverted the helicopters to the site. Upon arriving over the zone,

A company-size ARVN force moves away from its HMM-362 helicopter transports in an assault on Viet Cong positions in the Mekong Delta in July 1962.

the helicopters were greeted by an intense volume of enemy small-arms fire. The squadron commander's aircraft was hit several times, severing the rudder control and puncturing the main rotor transmission. Rathbun made a forced landing on a nearby road. Mechanics were quickly flown in, and the helicopter was repaired and returned to Soc Trang.

To provide protection for the helicopters, particularly during the critical landing and takeoff phases of operations, the squadron made a significant modification to its aircraft in August. It mounted M60 machine guns inside the cargo hatches on the starboard side of each helicopter. As the rules of engagement at this time clearly stated that U.S. forces could only fire in self-defense—defined as having been fired upon first—these machine guns could only be employed as a defensive measure. Nevertheless, as the helicopters were becoming exposed to increasing amounts of accurate enemy ground fire, the guns provided a much needed and welcome defense and fire suppression capability.

New Location, New Missions

As previously noted, when the first Marine helicopter squadron was deployed to Soc Trang in the southern region of South Vietnam, the USMACV commander had agreed that the Marine squadron would subsequently redeploy to Da Nang and replace the Army helicopter company there. The rationale for this move was twofold. First, the UH-34D's superior lift capability over the Army Piasecki CH-21 Shawnee—a tandem-rotor, "flying banana"—made it better suited for operations in the high mountain ranges in the northern I Corps area. Second, U.S. and SEATO contingency plans called for the Marine Corps to be employed in the northern parts of South Vietnam.

General Hawkins, the USMACV commander, had originally planned to send the Marine helicopter squadron to Da Nang on 1 August; however, appeals from the South Vietnamese III Corps commander and his senior U.S. advisor to scrap the squadron's departure altogether caused the general to slide the movement date to 15 September. Now, with August rushing to a close and September looming on the horizon, it appeared certain that the exchange of helicopter units would take place.

The switch was confirmed during the first days of September when General Hawkins directed Colonel Ireland

to prepare to deploy his helicopter task unit to Da Nang. Preparations had been made with the Army's 93d Helicopter Company at Da Nang to ensure the smooth transition of operations from the Army to the Marines. The move began on 4 September when Colonel Ireland dispatched an advance party of Marines from communications, utilities, fuel, and supply sections to make preparations to receive the task unit from Soc Trang.

Concurrently, HMM-163 continued to support a full schedule of commitments in the III Corps area. On 5 September, the squadron sustained its first casualty when three of its helicopters were hit by enemy small-arms fire and Corporal Billy S. Watson, a crew chief, was wounded. All three helicopters returned to Soc Trang safely, and the squadron continued to fly combat operations until the afternoon of 13 September, when support operations were terminated.

Early on 15 September, Marine Corps Hercules transports, which had arrived from Okinawa the previous day, began to carry the task unit's personnel, equipment, and supplies the 450 miles from Soc Trang to Da Nang. On the return trip, the transports carried the personnel, equipment, and supplies of the Army's 93d Helicopter Company. By day's end, much of the task unit's personnel and equipment had been moved. Colonel Rathbun's helicopters, pilots, and crews began their displacement on 16 September when 12 UH-34Ds made the seven-hour flight to Da Nang, stopping three times en route to refuel. The following day, while the remaining 12 helicopters were inbound, the first 12 UH-34Ds were executing operational commitments in support of South Vietnam's I Corps ground forces.

In I Corps, Shufly Marines would be supporting the 1st ARVN Division, with its headquarters at Hue, and the 2d ARVN Division, which was located at Da Nang. Major General Tran Van Don commanded both divisions. General Don's forces were occasionally augmented by elements of the 25th ARVN Division, which had its headquarters at Kontum in northwestern II Corps. Shufly Marines would also be facing a larger and more determined enemy force.

By early fall 1962, Viet Cong forces opposing the South Vietnamese and their American allies had grown to formidable strength. In I Corps, their numbers now included "four interprovincial battalions (main force), four interprovincial companies, five provincial companies, 18 district companies,

When a lift involved the permanent move of a Vietnamese unit, the Marine helicopter squadron transported all personal belongings—including live pigs, rice, and produce—of the moving unit.

and three district platoons." The Shufly Marines could count on increased opposition and hostile fire as they began their support of South Vietnamese forces in I Corps.

On 18 September, the helicopters of HMM-163 were back in action. That day, 14 UH-34Ds carried ARVN troops of the 2d Division in an uneventful troop lift that saw no enemy engagements. The following day, 10 helicopters were dispatched to a location 18 miles west of Da Nang to evacuate a threatened Vietnamese army outpost. When the helicopters departed the outpost, they carried everything with them that was not nailed down: people, pigs, cows, chickens and ducks, food, utensils, and personal belongings. In the coming months, as the enemy threat increased in I Corps, the frequency of these evacuations increased. On 26 September, 22 helicopters lifted two companies of Vietnamese Special Forces from Da Nang to a site some 45 miles south-southeast of the city and 15 miles south-southwest of Tam Ky. Hostile small-arms fire was encountered approaching the small, four-helicopter landing zone, resulting in hits to one aircraft.

Operations continued throughout the day, with a total of 428 troops lifted. Artillery had been employed in preparing the landing site, marking the first time that artillery had been used to support a Marine helicopter operation in South Vietnam.

On 6 October 1962, the Marine squadron suffered its first fatalities when a search-and-rescue helicopter carrying maintenance and medical personnel, and accompanying a 20-aircraft lift in support of 2d ARVN Division forces, crashed on a hillside 15 miles southeast of Tam Ky. Troops in accompanying helicopters were landed on the top and bottom of the hill, and a helicopter from Da Nang was dispatched to the site with medical and evacuation personnel. A doctor and a corpsman were lowered by hoist through 50- to 100-foot-tall trees into the crash site. They found that one pilot, the crew chief, five additional members of the task unit, and a Navy doctor and a corpsman had been killed. The other pilot was seriously injured.

HMM-163's missions evolved as the tour progressed. The

more mountainous terrain in I Corps, which was markedly different from the flatter terrain in III Corps to the south, in large measure, dictated how the helicopters could be employed. The terrain did not lend itself to the large-scale heliborne assaults that had been employed successfully in the delta. Further, the ARVN's mission in I Corps was different. The region served mostly as a link—a transit area—in the Viet Cong supply chain from the north and west to the south. To monitor and interdict these supply routes, the South Vietnamese military had established remote outposts in I Corps' mountainous, jungle-covered terrain. As a result, resupply, ARVN unit displacements, administrative movements, and logistic support soon were taking up more flight hours than those for combat-support troop lifts. Supporting these outposts required the Marine helicopter crews to fly routes that were channeled by the terrain and to land in zones that were small and frequently surrounded by dense jungle vegetation.

To adapt to this new environment, the squadron modified its flying techniques and took steps to improve the safety of its aircraft, crews, and passengers. With the terrain dictating the tactics used to approach and retire from landing zones, HMM-163 pilots approached their targets from behind masking terrain whenever possible, dropping into their designated zones with as much surprise as they could achieve. Subsequent runs into the same landing zone were made from alternate routes. Landing zones in close proximity to each other were approached simultaneously from opposite directions. While these tactics complicated the ability of escort aircraft to provide support, they enhanced the safety of the squadron's aircraft and crews.

In this new and more demanding environment, the selection and reconnaissance of landing sites took on new importance. Photographic reconnaissance of landing zones was begun, and the use of pathfinder or paratroop personnel to clear single landing zones was studied. As landing zones were usually small, the 300-meter distance between helicopter landing sites and trees—a flight policy enforced in the delta—was substantially reduced. Particular vigilance was required on the part of the pilots to recognize landing zones in which the Viet Cong had implanted wooden stakes to impale a helicopter as it landed. In instances where landing between the stakes was not possible, alternate landing zones were required.

Improved rescue techniques were developed, and a step beneath the door opening on the side of the helicopter allowed the hoist to be used at all times on all aircraft. Emergency rescue kits were devised. Marine pilots made nearly vertical descents into the landing zones and used evasive maneuvers, including maximum performance ascents during departure. They learned and adjusted to the reality that lifts at higher altitudes would accommodate only 6–9 ARVN soldiers, not the 11–12 soldiers per aircraft that had been lifted in the Mekong Delta.

Armor plating—recommended as the result of a study conducted while operating in the delta—was installed on all helicopters. It was attached beneath the clamshell engine compartment to provide protection to the vulnerable oil cooling systems. Installation of this armor plating meant that one fewer South Vietnamese soldier could be carried in each lift, but it was deemed a price well worth paying for the improved survivability.

Artillery and air strikes were often employed to prepare the landing zones, although in a postdeployment letter Colonel Rathbun reported that "I am not convinced of the effectiveness of saturation patterns by artillery or air strikes in jungle or heavily wooded areas." Air strikes were also employed to good advantage during landing operations. North American T-28 Trojans, Douglas AD-6 Skyraiders, and Douglas B-26 Invaders were frequently available. Ordnance loads varied by aircraft. AD-6 aircraft arrived on station with up to eight 500-pound general-purpose bombs, four 100-pound general-purpose bombs, and four .50-caliber machine guns. The T-28s carried a mix of 2.75-inch rockets, machine guns, and fragmentation bombs. A rapid response to support requests was ensured by stationing T-28s in racetrack patterns above both sides of inbound and landing helicopters. In one instance cited by Colonel Rathbun, T-28s flown by U.S. Air Force pilots with Vietnamese in the back seat were able to deliver .50-caliber machine-gun and rocket fire on insurgents firing on the Marine helicopters within 30 seconds of receiving the request.

The new year marked the end of HMM-163's deployment, and on 12 January 1963 Lieutenant Colonel Reinhardt Leu, commanding Marine Medium Helicopter Squadron 162 (HMM-162), relieved Colonel Rathbun. During its 163 days deployed to South Vietnam (the tour for helicopter squadrons had been lengthened from four to six months on the recommendation of Colonel Ireland), Rathbun's Ridge Runners had flown 15,200 sorties and 10,869 hours. In August 1962, HMM-163 had flown 2,543 hours—a record month. The squadron had lifted 25,216 combat assault troops and 59,024 other passengers, carried 2,228,776 pounds of cargo, and made 535 medical evacuations. Squadron aircraft had been hit by enemy fire 32 times. Although Colonel Rathbun would report that "the weather has been our nemesis during the past four months," his squadron had achieved a very impressive record of accomplishments.

In August 1963, as their Far East deployment was nearing its end, 44 of HMM-163's enlisted Marines learned that their service in South Vietnam had qualified them to receive and wear the combat aircrew insignia. When word of this was received, the squadron's officers elected to purchase the insignia for their crews and personally pin them on. In a late August ceremony at MCAF Futema, Okinawa, these 44 Marines—who ranged in grade from lance corporal to master sergeant—were awarded their insignias.

Laotian Crisis: May–August 1962

While U.S. combat support operations in South Vietnam were receiving the lion's share of the attention, the shadowy conflict in Laos was continuing unabated. As 1961 drew to a close, the fighting intensified between the royal Laotian forces and the Communist Pathet Lao. The pro-Western forces under the command of General Phoumi Nosavan were faring poorly against the Pathet Lao fighters, who were receiving support from the NVA, the Soviets, and the Chinese.

The continuing conflict in Laos had its genesis partly in North Vietnam's efforts—which violated the 1954 Geneva Agreement—to extend its control over the RVN. To further those efforts, it made incursions into Laos, and in the late 1950s it had begun providing military aid and training support to the Pathet Lao army of leftist Prince Souphanauvong. The Soviet Union had also begun to provide support. The United States' response to these activities was to initiate a military assistance program for the anti-Communist government of Prince Boun Oum. This assistance did little to blunt the Pathet Lao's advances.

As noted previously, Pathet Lao forces seized two Laotian provinces in the country's northeast in early 1960. Augmented

by NVA forces, they were poised to continue their aggression further to the west, which would place the administrative capital of Vientiane and the royal capital of Luang Prabang at risk. In early 1961, the Pathet Lao and NVA attacked the strategically located Plain of Jars. By March, the Pathet Lao held the plain and with it the town of Xiengkhouang and its airport. President Kennedy ordered CinCPac to send U.S. military units to Thailand to support Air America pilots who were flying in support of the pro-Western Laotian government. Concurrently, the Kennedy administration employed diplomatic channels to secure Soviet assistance in arranging a cease-fire. The situation cooled somewhat when 14 nations agreed to reconvene the conference at Geneva to consider the neutralization of the Kingdom of Laos.

The Geneva Conference, which included the United States, the Soviet Union, Communist China, and North Vietnam, opened on 16 May 1961. The opening of the conference and the cease-fire returned the façade of stability to Laos. However, the conference moved at an agonizingly slow pace, and while it did allow the United States some temporary breathing room—the Kennedy administration ended the alert of its forces in the Pacific—it did not bring peace to the Kingdom of Laos. In fact, violations of the cease-fire began as soon as it was announced and continued through the end of 1961 and into 1962. The Pathet Lao and the North Vietnamese, with the support of the Soviet Union and Communist China, continued to make gains on the ground that would enhance their bargaining position—and the final outcome—at the Geneva Conference. When the conferees signed the Declaration of Neutrality of Laos in Geneva on 23 July 1962, the Kingdom of Laos was no closer to peace or neutrality than it was before the conference.

During the first months of 1962, heavy fighting resumed in Laos. Backed by the forces of their North Vietnamese ally, the Pathet Lao routed General Phouma's major government units from Nam Tha, a town on the eastern bank of the Mekong River in northwestern Laos. Phouma's forces retreated to the southwest in disarray, crossing the Mekong River into Thailand with the Pathet Lao and North Vietnamese forces seemingly poised to continue their pursuit. With the territorial integrity of Thailand (a SEATO member) threatened and America's efforts at Geneva enjoying scant success, the Kennedy administration decided it was time to

BLT 3/9 Marines, newly arrived from Okinawa, stage on the dock at Klong Toey, Bangkok, after disembarking from amphibious ships. The USS *Navarro* (APA 215), USS *Point Defiance* (LSD 31), and the USS *Valley Forge* (LPH 8) transported the team from Okinawa to Thailand.

make a strong response: American forces would return to Thailand in much larger numbers than before.

Forces Assemble and Deploy

In response to the deteriorating situation in Laos, President Kennedy ordered U.S. forces deployed to Thailand. Admiral Felt activated a task force headquarters—Joint Task Force 116 (JTF 116)—and assigned Major General John Condon, commanding general of 1st MAW, as its commander. JTF 116 consisted primarily of Marine air and ground units, with the Army and Air Force fleshing out the remainder of the force. Now, in the face of a once again deteriorating situation in Southeast Asia, the JCS directed Admiral Felt to upgrade the readiness posture of JTF 116 and prepare it for deployment. In concurrent actions, Admiral Felt replaced General Condon, installing Lieutenant General John L. Richardson,

USA, then serving as deputy commander in chief of U.S. Army Forces Pacific, as commander, Joint Task Force 116 (CJTF 116). The president then directed Richardson to execute CinCPac operation plan 32-59 (OPLAN 32-59) Phase II (Laos). Admiral Felt further directed the general "to act in such a way that would leave no doubt as to American intentions to defend Thailand." Further, Richardson was to position his forces so that they could respond to any Communist military threat to Thailand. It was expected that the execution of these orders would diminish the ongoing warfare in Laos.

OPLAN 32-59 called for a Marine expeditionary brigade to deploy to an airfield and cantonment in the vicinity of Udorn, Thailand, a provincial capital located 350 miles northeast of Bangkok. Plans called for the MEB to consist of a regimental landing team of three infantry battalions with attachments, a provisional air group consisting of a Marine jet attack squadron, a Marine helicopter transport squadron and attachments, and various supporting units. To lead this organization, Brigadier General Ormond R. Simpson, the assistant division commander of 3d MarDiv, was designated as Naval Component Commander 116/Commanding General, 3d MEB. In 1985, then-Lieutenant General Simpson remarked, "There's not a T/O for a brigade, it can be whatever you decide it to be. . . . Had we taken in what we originally planned to do, it would have numbered over 7,000."

General Simpson's organization never grew to full brigade size. As the operation plan was being executed and the MEB was in the process of deploying and establishing itself in Thailand, the crisis in Laos began to show signs of abating. In light of this, the decision was made to provide the MEB with only the single infantry battalion that had already been assigned, to shrink the size of the air group, and to furnish only some of the combat support elements provided for in the T/O of the CJTF 116 Operation Plan. As Simpson recalled, "Negotiations were such that they put a clamp on the number of U.S. forces in there, so by that time I had 3,500 and never got any more than 3,500. It was a sort of lopsided outfit, but it was pretty well organized. We had a full battalion landing team, we had a Marine helicopter squadron of 20 aircraft, we had 18 A4s [Douglas A4 Skyhawks]. We did not have, as it turned out, enough engineering support to do what we had to do." In light of its diminished size, the expeditionary brigade was redesignated a Marine expeditionary unit.

On 10 May 1962, CinCPac placed forces designated for JTF 116 in Defense Condition 3 and directed that they be deployed to advance locations to increase the JTF's readiness posture. The forces to be assigned included a brigade headquarters, a headquarters company with a communications detachment, a battalion landing team, a provisional Marine aircraft group, and a logistics support group. The actual units assigned were scattered over the Western Pacific and would have to be quickly brought together in Thailand to form a cohesive, combat-ready fighting force. The infantry battalion, Battalion Landing Team 3/9 (BLT 3/9), and the Marine helicopter squadron, Marine Medium Helicopter Squadron 261 (HMM-261), were afloat in the Gulf of Thailand undergoing training as part of the U.S. Seventh Fleet's Special Landing Force. Marine Attack Squadron 332 (VMA-332) was located at MCAF Iwakuni, Japan. These units were directed to begin movement to Udorn. The logistics support group and the additional elements of the provisional Marine aircraft group would be assembled from units and unit detachments in Japan and on Okinawa and then sent to Thailand.

On 14 May, the 20 A4D-2N Skyhawks of VMA-332, commanded by Lieutenant Colonel Harvey M. Patton, departed MCAF Iwakuni for Naval Air Station Cubi Point in the Philippines. After a stop to refuel at Naha, Okinawa, all planes arrived at Cubi Point later the same day. At 0700 on 16 May, the squadron departed the Philippines for Udorn, Thailand. With an in-flight refueling by Hercules tankers approximately 100 miles west of Cubi Point, all aircraft completed the 1,070–nautical mile flight and landed safely at Udorn by 1200 the same day. Because no arrangements had been made for their arrival, Air America personnel assisted the pilots in erecting tents on frames that had been constructed by MABS-16 Marines the previous year. The Joint U.S. Military Advisory Group detachment and the Royal Thai Army provided assistance with transportation. Support elements from MABS-12, MATCU-66, Marine Air Control Squadron 4 (MACS-4), and HMM-261 began arriving from

Marines move out after disembarking from their amphibious transports. Royal Thai Army vehicles carried the Marines from the harbor to Bangkok's Don Muang Airport where they were flown to Udorn in northeast Thailand.

Defense Department (Marine Corps) A182833

Marines erect a sign on 20 May 1962 to identify their headquarters near the airfield at Udorn, Thailand. U.S.-Thai negotiations early in the deployment so limited the number of Marines that would be allowed to enter Thailand that the sign had to be changed from the 3d MEB to the 3d MEU

Iwakuni on 18 May. A total of 30 GV-1s and two C-124s were required to complete the lift. Flight operations began at Udorn on 19 May.

On 17 May, the USS *Navarro* (APA 215) and the USS *Point Defiance* (LSD 31) arrived pier side at Bangkok harbor and at 0800 began off-loading BLT 3/9. The latter ship carried the bulk of Lieutenant Colonel Harold W. Adams's 1,500-man BLT 3/9. As BLT 3/9's Marines, sailors, equipment, and supplies were off-loaded, they were transported by Thai trucks to Bangkok's Don Muang Airport and then airlifted by U.S. Air Force C-130 and C-124 transport aircraft directly to Udorn. The movement, which began at approximately 1200 on 17 May, was completed by 1600 on 20 May, employing 84 C-130 and C-124 transport flights. Class I supplies (subsistence), Class II supplies (clothing, individual equipment, tools, weapons), a 5-day supply of Class III supplies (petroleum, oils, and lubricants), a contingency package of Class IV supplies (construction materials), a 3-day supply of Class V

supplies (ammunition), and Class VI supplies (major items including vehicles) were also moved by air. The remainder, which included all remaining Class II, IV, and V supplies and train guards, was moved by rail.

The shallow harbor required the USS *Valley Forge* (LPH 8) to anchor in the stream. Soon thereafter, the first wave of HMM-261's UH-34D helicopters departed the ship and began arriving at Don Muang at approximately 0530. They carried approximately 400 members of BLT 3/9, plus their own personnel and selected equipment. Off-loading of the major portions of the combat elements was completed by 1700. HMM-261 flew its 18 UH-34Ds from Don Muang Airport to Korat, where they refueled before continuing on to Udorn. The squadron was operationally ready on 19 May.

The 3d Marine Expeditionary Unit (3d MEU) headquarters, initially consisting of 25 officers and 72 enlisted personnel, was airlifted from Okinawa to Udorn on 19 May. Accompanied by a detachment of the 1st Communication

The billeting and work spaces for the 3d MEU headquarters element were located near Udorn's 6,000-foot-long, 150-foot-wide, hard-surface airfield.

Company (Provisional), the headquarters element flew directly to Udorn, stopping only at Clark Air Base in the Philippines to refuel. The command element arrived the same day, and, on 20 May, General Simpson took command of all U.S. Marine and Navy units at Udorn. The 3d MEU air-ground team had been officially established.

On 19 May, Marine Hercules refueler-transports began airlifting aviation support elements from Okinawa to Udorn. These included detachments from MACSs-2 and -4, MABS-12, and a provisional Marine aircraft group (Prov MAG) headquarters. Upon landing, Colonel Ross S. Mickey, the Prov MAG commanding officer, established his headquarters at the airfield and assumed operational command of all Marine aviation elements. Two tank landing ships (LSTs) brought the remainder of the Prov MAG to Thailand. The USS *Vernon County* (LST 1161) began loading at Okinawa on 21 May and sailed the following day. The USS *Windham County* (LST 1170) commenced loading on 28 May and sailed on 30 May.

In addition to carrying the major elements of MACS-4 and MABS-12, the *Windham County* also carried approximately 625 tons of ammunition. The *Vernon County* arrived pier side in Bangkok harbor on 2 June and was followed six days later by the *Windham County*. Off-loading began immediately, and the Prov MAG's equipment and supplies were transferred to awaiting trains. The first rail shipment of 20 cars arrived at Udorn on 11 June and was followed by 20- and 14-car trains that arrived on 12 and 13 June, respectively.

Planning for the logistics support group had been initiated concurrently with the activation of the expeditionary unit's headquarters, and an advance party of the logistics support group had deployed to Udorn with the 3d MEU headquarters. The remainder of the group included Lieutenant Colonel Robert S. Hudson, its commanding officer; 23 officers; and 487 enlisted Marines who were organized into a motor transport detachment, a medical detachment, a supply unit, and an engineer detachment. On 1 June, the logistics support

The construction of above-ground platforms became the main priority as Marines raced to have their camp built before the monsoon rains arrived in late June. Once the platforms were completed, the Marines constructed frames to support their general purpose tents.

In this small section of the 3d MEU's cantonment at Udorn, Thailand, the general purpose tents were spread across a wooden frame and then anchored securely to the wooden deck. The frame provided stability for the tents against the monsoon winds.

group began staging its equipment at Naha, Okinawa's major port, and it began loading the three awaiting Navy ships—the USS *Whitfield County* (LST 1169), USS *Washtenaw County* (LST 1166), and USS *Mathews* (AKA 96)—the following day. Once loaded, all ships sailed south, arriving at Bangkok by 10 June. Unloading began on 12 June and was completed in three days. The logistics support group's 120 pieces of equipment and 235 tons of supplies moved from Bangkok to Udorn by rail. Its Marines flew with the last contingent, boarding aircraft from Don Muang Airport at 1400 on 16 June and arriving at Udorn two hours later. The deployment to Thailand required approximately 9 ships, 310 airlifts, and 270 rail cars.

Camp Locations and Construction

Early in the deployment, the command decided that two camps would be required. The 3d MEU's headquarters, air elements, and logistics support group would be billeted and have their work spaces located adjacent to the Udorn airfield. BLT 3/9 would establish a separate camp nearby. Initially, both camps would be established on the ground.

BLT 3/9 established its camp near the town of Nong Ta Kai, eight miles south of Udorn, near the railroad and on the main supply route. This site, initially thought to be its temporary cantonment, turned out to be the best choice for its permanent camp. It was on high ground—above the level that water would rise to during the approaching monsoon season—and it had good drainage. Only pallets would be required for flooring in the tents. It was also reasonably close to the airfield and the 3d MEU headquarters.

Some elements of the Marine expeditionary unit located in the vicinity of the Udorn airfield were not so fortunate. Information acquired from the previous year (as noted earlier, MABS-16's cantonment had been adjacent to the airfield during its March–October 1961 deployment to Udorn) indicated that the relatively flat area around the airfield would be flooded up to a depth of 30 inches during the monsoon season. In a May meeting with the provincial governor, General Simpson had been told that he had "40 days to build a camp" before the monsoon rains began. To build a camp above flood levels would require that all structures—billeting, mess halls, working, and storage—sit on platforms raised approximately three feet above the ground.

Immediately upon arrival, the race began to complete construction of the elevated areas before the onset of the monsoon rains that typically begin in late June. The 3d Platoon, Company C, 3d Pioneer Battalion, that was attached to BLT 3/9, began building the day it arrived. Once its advance elements arrived, Company C, 7th Engineer Battalion, assumed overall responsibility for the construction of shelters for billeting, equipment, and supplies. In spite of these efforts, however, it soon became evident that they would be unable to complete their tasks in the time available. Without additional help, 3d MEU's cantonments would not be off the ground before the monsoons arrived.

To assist in the construction effort, General Simpson requested the support of a U.S. Navy Construction Battalion (Seabee) detachment. His request was quickly approved and, on 27 May, Detachment Zulu, Naval Mobile Construction Battalion 10 (NMCB-10), consisting of 2 officers and 69 enlisted men, was authorized to deploy to Udorn for 60 days to support construction efforts. Transported by C-130 aircraft, the detachment arrived at Udorn on 31 May. However, the Seabees did not come without a price. To keep within his authorized numbers, General Simpson was required to identify a like number of Marines and ship them out of Thailand. The Marines departed on the same aircraft that brought the Seabees to Udorn.

Detachment Zulu was assigned the task of preparing all of the construction materials needed to build the camps. It established a sawmill area for receiving and cutting lumber and began prefabricating the structures, including the platforms and tent frames. The detachment then developed plans for constructing mess halls, equipment platforms, utility platforms, walkways, heads, and other special requirements. As the Seabees prepared the materials, the Marine engineers built the camps.

All construction materials were procured locally. Initially, the Thai lumberyards were slow to respond to the 3d MEU's requirements. However, seven sawmills—all within 50 miles of Udorn—were soon devoting their entire output to the construction of the two Marine camps.

The accomplishments of Company C, 7th Engineer Battalion; Detachment Zulu, NMCB-10; the 3d Platoon, Company C, 3d Pioneer Battalion; and the Marines of MABS-12, Sub-Unit One, were nothing short of amazing. Together, these units constructed 310 platforms that were 16 feet by 32 feet, 302 platforms that were 96 feet by 108 feet, 5 mess halls, 7 heads, and several other structures. In addition, they constructed more than a mile of walkways. All of these structures were built aboveground and out of reach of the anticipated monsoon floods.

Of the myriad tasks calling for Company C, 7th Engineer Battalion's attention, road repair and construction, particularly near the airfield, was an urgent requirement. Even before the monsoon season, rain could quickly turn any dirt road into a muddy, impassable quagmire. Employing borrowed and rented equipment from a civilian construction company with contracts in the area—nearly all of the engineer company's equipment was en route and did not arrive until about 16 June—the company made road repair and construction a priority.

Approximately three miles of roadway were raised and surfaced with laterite (low-grade decomposed iron ore plentiful in northeast Thailand), and maintenance—which would continue throughout the deployment—was begun on an additional eight miles of roads in the vicinity of the airfield. An additional three-quarters of a mile of roadway was graded and drained in the BLT 3/9 cantonment area. To provide access to the ammunition storage site, which was constructed 10 miles south of BLT 3/9's cantonment, the engineers raised two roads. Each road was approximately 20 feet wide and 1,000 feet long and surfaced with laterite. In addition, the engineers built and installed four large box culverts, a personnel bridge, and a 20-ton wooden vehicular bridge.

Construction of the ammunition storage area was a major project on its own. A two-million-square-foot area was cleared of brush and stumps, and six storage pads were raised and surfaced with laterite. Wood frame shelters were then constructed for each pad and covered with either canvas or tin roofing.

The 3d MEU's Roles and Missions
In his special report, General Simpson noted that "the role and mission of the 3d Marine Expeditionary Unit in Thailand was unusual in many respects." The assigned mission was to serve as a "show of force" and to be prepared for other operations as directed. Simpson viewed the unit's mission in somewhat different terms. He saw the Marine deployment to

Defense Department (Marine Corps) A182901

BGen Ormond R. Simpson speaks with Under Secretary of the Navy Paul B. Fay Jr. during a visit to the 3d MEU's cantonment on 30 June 1962. Simpson is wearing the utility uniform that he reported to be "totally unsuited for operations in SEAsia."

Thailand as both the application of an "Instrument of Diplomacy" and as the application of an "Instrument of Power." In the former, he was pleased to note that the people of northeast Thailand greeted the arrival of his Marines with a sense of "gratification, wonderment, and some initial apprehension." He believed that it was important to "sell the Marines to the Thais" and sell them he did. Soon after his arrival, the general met with the governor of Udorn Province, the lord mayor of Udorn, and other province and city officials. To reinforce his message, Simpson was accompanied by his information service officer and the local public affairs officer from the U.S. Information Service office. The meeting went very well, and an understanding and mutual friendship were established that remained throughout 3d MEU's stay.

Both the governor and the mayor assured the 3d MEU commander that the Thai people were very happy that the Marines were there and wished to assist them in any way possible. Over time, this assistance translated into cooperation in law enforcement, price controls, and civil affairs. For their part, the Marines engaged in a number of people-to-people programs: they cleared plots of land for playgrounds

The king of Thailand, Ab Adulyodej Bhumibol, addresses the Marines of BLT 3/9 during his visit to their camp on 15 June 1962. Also in attendance (from left) were U.S. Ambassador to Thailand Kenneth Todd Young Jr., BGen Ormond Simpson, and Queen Sirikit (on the platform with umbrella).

and soccer fields; repaired the screening and electrical wiring of a local orphanage; screened a porch; and constructed a new sleeping area. In addition, many conversational English language programs were started. The mutual respect, understanding, and support between the Thai population and the Marines could be seen in the fact that no adverse incidents of any consequence were reported during the two-and-a-half-month deployment and total claims against the U.S. Government amounted to less than $50.

As for the "Instrument of Power" element of its mission, the 3d MEU proved adroit in both planning and execution. In response to its assigned mission to "be prepared for such other operations as directed," the unit had completely settled in Udorn by 15 June and "was prepared in all respects for sustained combat operations, if required." OPLAN 1-62 directed

the movement of BLT 3/9 troops to previously selected positions and roadblocks from which they could guard the Udorn airfield complex against enemy ground attack and guerrilla activity.

In light of the less-than-stable situation in Laos, General Simpson directed that a 3d MEU operation plan be drafted and promulgated. Its basic provision was to task certain units with the seizure and defense of Wattay Airfield near Vientiane if the situation should ever require it. The Marines were ready for any eventuality and were training in the geographical areas they would be called upon to fight in if the situation in Laos took a turn for the worse.

Of the many visits by dignitaries to the 3d MEU during its deployment in Thailand, none was more impressive than the one made by Thailand's king, Ab Adulyodej Bhumibol, and his wife, Queen Sirikit, who visited the camp on 15 June. They arrived in a Royal Thai Air Force Douglas DC-3. Several senior Thai military officers accompanied the king and queen, as did the U.S. ambassador to Thailand, Kenneth Todd Young Jr. A simple reviewing stand was constructed from which the king and queen viewed an air show arranged by General Simpson. The king addressed the Marines who had been assembled for his visit, and then the royal couple toured the camp in a Thai government Rolls Royce Rover.

Although the Thai Army chief of staff had told General Simpson to "just drive them through the camp," the general had other plans. He had prepared a billeting tent to a very high state of cleanliness, and he wanted to show it to the king and queen. As their car approached the tent, the general—who was sitting behind the king and queen—asked if they would like to see a "typical billeting tent." At their consent, Simpson led them through the tent. Although their visit lasted only two hours, the general orchestrated it so that as many of his Marines as possible were able to see the royal couple.

Training in Thailand

Training began immediately upon 3d MEU's arrival. In light of the unit's mission, the training took on increased significance and focused on accomplishing specific objectives. The first objective was to execute its show-of-force mission, which was largely to impress the Pathet Lao and their Communist supporters with the combat power of the Marine expeditionary unit. Training provided the 3d MEU with the best venue to display the greatest number of Marines, their combat power, and their superior weaponry and equipment. The second objective was to acclimatize the Marines to the oppressive heat and humidity extant in northeast Thailand (and Southeast Asia, in general). The third objective was to become completely familiar with the area and its jungle terrain.

To ensure that all three objectives would be met, VMA-332 and HMM-261 flew reconnaissance and orientation missions, while BLT 3/9 conducted motorized and foot marches. The first air-ground exercise was conducted on 26 May, only six days after General Simpson assumed command. HMM-261's UH-34Ds lifted a company of BLT 3/9 Marines to landing zones near Nong Han. A-4D Skyhawks

from VMA-332 flew helicopter escort missions and simulated preparation of landing zones. Training exercises of this nature continued until the Prov MAG was withdrawn. Then North American F-100 Super Sabre aircraft from the Air Force component of JTF 116 and the tactical air control party from BLT 3/9 engaged in close air support techniques.

On 6 June 1962, the commanding general of 3d MEU was assigned the additional task of providing training to the Thai Border Patrol Police located at Udorn and Ubon, a town to the south. This additional task provided a rare opportunity for Marines to both extend training assistance and to train with the paramilitary forces of another country. Two reinforced BLT 3/9 platoons were assigned the mission, which included instruction on individual and crew served weapons, map and compass reading, sanitation and field hygiene, and small unit tactics at the squad and platoon levels. Language problems proved minimal and were in large measure overcome by the use of visual training aids and interpreters. In addition to fostering a mutual understanding between the Thai and American forces, the training also afforded 3d MEU the opportunity to contribute to the preservation and integrity of the Thai border.

The amount of training accomplished by 3d MEU's subordinate commands during their brief stay in northeast Thailand was impressive. Its attack squadron—VMA-332 with 20 A-4D-2N Skyhawks assigned—averaged 20–25 sorties a day for the entire period. The medium helicopter squadron, HMM-261, flew more than 1,000 hours and carried 3,106 passengers and 102,760 pounds of cargo with 18 UH-34Ds. MATCU-66 controlled 3,003 aircraft arrivals, 525 instrument approaches, and 502 instrument departures. BLT 3/9 trained at the squad, platoon, and company levels in more than 18,000 square miles of unfamiliar terrain and conducted a detailed reconnaissance of the area's roads and bridges. Extensive foot, motorized, and heliborne patrols, lasting from a few hours to four days, were conducted by BLT 3/9 Marines and Navy corpsmen. As evidenced by the sheer amount of training, the Marines deployed with 3d MEU took many opportunities to test their skills. Moreover, the combat power displayed during the training exercises—the "show of force" element of the 3d MEU mission—was not lost on the Pathet Lao and their supporters on the north side of the Mekong River.

Marines from Company L, BLT 3/9, muster prior to boarding a U.S. Air Force C-130 Hercules for their return from Thailand to Okinawa.

While in northeast Thailand, Marines trained and worked in the standard Marine Corps utility uniform. In his special report, General Simpson criticized this uniform as "totally unsuited for operations in Southeast Asia." He noted that it was "unbearably hot" and that its tight weave did not allow air to circulate to the body. Moreover, when it got wet, it was very slow to dry due to the high humidity of the area. "If Marines are to work effectively for long periods of time in areas such as northeast Thailand," the general concluded, "a better answer than our current utility uniform is required."

The 3d MEU Withdraws

The Geneva talks had languished since their inception, particularly while Communist forces were enjoying success in Laos. This situation reversed somewhat and the crisis abated as the U.S. joint task force—with the 3d MEU as a major combat element—established itself on the ground in northeast Thailand in May 1962. As the 3d MEU settled in and the United States' resolve became apparent, American diplomats in Geneva and Vientiane began reporting progress in their

negotiations. Communist forces halted their advance short of the Thai border. In light of these encouraging signs, President Kennedy directed on 29 June that major elements of American combat forces be withdrawn from Thailand.

The 3d MEU's operations (i.e., camp construction and training) had been based on the expectation that its deployment to Thailand would be for an indefinite period of time. However, the Marines were fully prepared to change course on a moment's notice. Consequently, when General Richardson directed General Simpson on 29 June to prepare for the immediate withdrawal of a major portion of his expeditionary unit, the Marines were prepared. The Prov MAG, consisting of HMM-162, VMA-332, the MABS-12 subunit, and MACS-4, would be withdrawn first, as would one company from BLT 3/9. The complete withdrawal of these units was not expected to begin before 2 July, but was to be completed within one week once the order was given.

On 1 July, HMM-162 displaced from Udorn and staged its helicopters, personnel, and equipment at Don Muang Airport in Bangkok. On 2 July, they landed on board the USS

Valley Forge. Eighteen of VMA-332's Skyhawks departed the Udorn airfield on 2 July and, after refueling from Marine Hercules tankers in the vicinity of Da Nang, continued on to Cubi Point. The remaining two A-4Ds joined them the following day. Slightly more than 100 lifts employing GV-1/C-130 and C-124 transports were required to move the remainder of the withdrawing force. Fifty flights carried the personnel, supplies, and equipment of MACS-4 and MATCU-66 to Don Muang where they were trucked to the Bangkok harbor and loaded on board the waiting USS *Carter Hall* (LSD 3) and the USS *Belle Grove* (LSD 2) for surface movement to Cubi Point. An additional 50-plus lifts carried the remaining assets of the Prov MAG to Cubi Point. Of these, Marine Hercules flew 52 lifts, employing 5 aircraft. The provisional group had withdrawn 829 personnel, 303 vehicles, and 2.4 million pounds of cargo. Three lifts were required to carry Company L, BLT 3/9, from Udorn directly to Okinawa. By 6 July, 3d MEU had been reduced by over 1,000 men.

With the departure of the Prov MAG and the BLT 3/9 rifle company, 3d MEU was reduced to a headquarters and service company, a communications detachment, a logistics support unit, and a battalion landing team minus one company. Training continued and, with the onset of the rainy season, a second major reconnaissance of northeast Thailand's roads was made to ascertain differences in their trafficability during this season. Overall, however, the tempo of operations declined. Construction projects were limited to building only what was essential to continue operations and improve the habitability of the camps. R&R flights to Bangkok were initiated, and approximately 20 Marines and sailors were shuttled south each day to enjoy 48 hours of liberty in Thailand's capital city. JTF 116 provided an Army de Havilland Canada CV-2A Caribou cargo plane to assist the 3d MEU with its administrative requirements.

In the early weeks of July, reports from Geneva projected the likelihood that an agreement would soon be forthcoming, and General Richardson was directed to prepare for the withdrawal of the remaining forces in Thailand. On 23 July 1962, the 14 nations assembled at Geneva signed a Declaration on the Neutrality of Laos. Previously, the warring factions in Laos had agreed to form a coalition government to administer the soon-to-be neutral country that would be headed by Prince Souvanna Phouma. The declaration committed the 14

signatories to recognize and respect the sovereignty, independence, and neutrality of the Kingdom of Laos. Further, it prohibited foreign troops from entering or operating anywhere in the country. All of these provisions would be flagrantly and repeatedly violated by the North Vietnamese and their supporters as the war in South Vietnam escalated and the NVA constructed and employed routes through Laos (called the Ho Chi Minh Trail by Americans) to funnel troops, munitions, and supplies to their forces in the south.

On 21 July, General Simpson was directed to submit requirements for the withdrawal of all Marine elements from Thailand and to have all Marines out of the country within 96 hours of the order to execute. The decision was made to leave all Class I and Class III supplies behind in Udorn. All ammunition supplies would be withdrawn, initially by rail to Bangkok, and then by ship to their final destination. The remaining elements of BLT 3/9 would be airlifted first, followed by the headquarters company and the communications detachment. Concurrently, the logistics support group, minus Detachment Zulu, NMCB-10, would be moved by rail and air to Bangkok for loading on board ships. Once on board, they would sail to Okinawa.

The order to initiate the second phase of 3d MEU's withdrawal was received at 1115 (local time) on 28 July. Twenty minutes later, the first Hercules departed Udorn, and by 31 July—approximately 27 hours ahead of its 96-hour deadline—36 GV-1/C-130 lifts had completed the withdrawal of all of 3d MEU's combat troops. With staging and movement control teams in place, the remainder of the retrograde operation was executed smoothly. The first train with the 3d MEU's equipment and supplies departed Udorn on 31 July, with the final train departing for Bangkok on 4 August. In all, 192 flatbed cars and 90 boxcars were required in the second phase to move the remaining equipment, supplies, and vehicles. Five ships—one AKA, two LSDs, and two LSTs—were required to transport the cargo to Okinawa.

General Simpson and his headquarters staff departed Udorn for Bangkok on 3 August. Four days later, operational control of 3d MEU was passed by CJTF 116 to the commander of Task Force 79 on Okinawa. The commanding general and his staff departed Bangkok and arrived on Okinawa the same day. The ships returned to Okinawa, and all were off-loaded by 15 August. The 3d MEU headquarters

Vietnamese marines improved their mobility by using small boats when operating on the rivers and canals in the Mekong Delta.

completed its administrative details and was deactivated on 31 August 1962.

Marine Advisors and the Vietnamese Marine Corps: 1963–64

The South Vietnamese marines continued serving as a part of Saigon's general reserve and under the direct control of the Vietnamese Joint General Staff in the early months of 1963. Three VNMC battalions were garrisoned in small, basically unimproved camps around the town of Tu Duc just north of Saigon. The recently formed artillery battalion became fully operational in mid-January and was also garrisoned near Tu Duc. The 4th Battalion was located on the coast at Vung Tau. While the VNMC battalions spent most of their time away from their camps on operations, Saigon normally held one battalion back near Tu Duc ready to respond to emergencies.

The Marine Advisory Division, still commanded by Lieutenant Colonel Clarence G. Moody Jr., lost five enlisted billets in April (the first sergeant's billet and the four assistant infantry advisor billets). No officer billets were lost, and the advisory division was able to provide a commissioned officer advisor to every major operational VNMC command.

Two major improvements—one in operations and one in training—were effected by the VNMC in 1963. The first was the return to multibattalion combat operations, which allowed Lieutenant Colonel Le Nguyen Khang, the brigade commander, to employ the provisional marine brigade's headquarters. No brigade-level operations had been undertaken since 1960. In 1963, the Vietnamese Marine Brigade conducted three multibattalion operations, but the results would not justify the efforts and manpower expended.

The first operation began in the first week of the new year with Colonel Khang leading two marine infantry battalions in an amphibious landing near the tip of the Ca Mau Peninsula. The brigade's mission was to clear Viet Cong units from a series of villages in support of the Strategic Hamlet Program. Elaborate precautions had been taken—including sailing the entire landing force out of sight of land for two days—to keep secret the location of the objective area. Nonetheless, when the 2d Battalion, advised by Captain Richard B. Taylor, and the 4th Battalion, advised by Captain Don R. Christensen, came ashore from their landing ships, they found few guerrillas to fight. The villages were largely deserted, and Colonel Moody noted that "they had taken everything, even the cattle and the other livestock." The operation had clearly been compromised. The action resulted in only 11 Viet Cong killed and 14 wounded. The cost to the Vietnamese marines was 5 men killed and 14 wounded, mostly from snipers and booby traps. Colonel Khang took his headquarters and the 4th Battalion back to Saigon. The 2d Battalion remained and conducted security operations until 11 April 1963.

In the second multibattalion offensive, which began in late April, the Vietnamese marines attacked Do Xa, a major Viet Cong base camp area that had never before been entered by government forces. Located where the borders of Quang Tin, Quang Ngai, and Kontum Provinces met, the Do Xa area had been under Communist control since the early days of the French-Indochina War. The scheme of maneuver was fairly simple. Employing U.S. Marine and Army helicopters, elements of the ARVN 2d and 25th Divisions would be helilifted to sites surrounding Do Xa to establish a cordon around the area. The provisional Vietnamese Marine Brigade would then be helilifted into the center of the area to search for Communist camps.

The initial deployment of forces was executed without incident. The 2d Battalion, with Captain Taylor, was trucked to the Tam Ky airstrip and then lifted into the objective area some 30 miles southwest of the capital. Advancing by motor march, Colonel Khang established his command post in the vicinity of the small, ARVN-held town of Tra My, about 24 miles southwest of Tam Ky. The 75mm pack-howitzer battery, advised by Major Croft, and the 4th Battalion, advised by Captain Christensen, accompanied the brigade commander and provided security. In a repeat of the brigade's amphibious landing on the Ca Mau Peninsula, where the Vietnamese marines discovered a major camp, they found this one to also be deserted. During extensive patrolling for two weeks after the initial assaults, neither the ARVN nor the Vietnamese marines encountered a major opposing force. Once again, the Viet Cong had been alerted, probably by the initial movement of ARVN forces into the area. When the

operation ended in mid-May, the VNMC returned to their camps north of Saigon.

In the third brigade-size operation, three Vietnamese marine battalions joined with ARVN, VNAF, and Vietnamese Navy units in a search-and-clear operation in Gia Dinh Province, about 20 miles southeast of Saigon. As was the case with the previous two operations, Communist forces successfully eluded their attackers, and government forces failed to engage enemy forces of any appreciable size. The operation in Gia Dinh Province ended on 1 November 1963, with inconclusive results.

The second major improvement (training) came late in the year when the Vietnamese Joint General Staff approved the establishment of a separate training facility for the Vietnamese marines. The VNMC would no longer have to rely on the ARVN for its recruits. VNMC engineers, advised by Captain Robert C. Jones, constructed a small training facility at Thu Duc. To staff the facility, Colonel Moody arranged for a small number of VNMC noncommissioned officers to travel to the Marine Corps Recruit Training Center at San Diego to train as drill instructors.

President Diem Assassinated

The government of President Ngo Dinh Diem was not faring any better. After some relatively peaceful early years, the Diem government began to experience dissent in 1959. Political opposition significantly increased, stimulated partly by the August 1959 elections in which Diem's chosen candidates won every seat in the National Assembly. A failed coup in November 1960 served only to highlight Diem's increasing unpopularity. Senior military officers privately began to express disapproval with Diem's handling of the war. Religious opposition to the Catholic-run government grew, highlighted from June to October 1963 by the highly publicized self-immolations of several Buddhist monks. President Diem and his brother, Ngo Dinh Nhu, staged reprisal raids on Buddhist temples throughout the country, some of which they tried to blame on the nation's generals.

On 1 November 1963, a military junta led by ARVN Major General Duong Van Minh staged a coup d'état that overthrew the government and resulted in the deaths of President Diem and his brother Ngo Dinh Nhu. With the South Vietnamese 2d Marine Battalion blocking a major highway into Saigon that prevented military units loyal to the president from intervening, the 1st and 4th Marine Battalions moved into the city to participate in the coup. Fighting continued into the early hours of 2 November, when the 4th Marine Battalion attacked and captured the presidential palace. The fighting cost the lives of 4 South Vietnamese marines and 12 others were wounded. No U.S. Marine advisors were involved in the fighting. They had been alerted by Lieutenant Colonel Wesley L. Noren, who directed them to remain in their quarters.

When the power struggle was over, the military units returned to fighting the war. In the remaining two months of 1963, the VNMC engaged in several operations of short duration. During the second week of November, the 2d Marine Battalion, accompanied by Captain James P. McWilliams, participated with the 11th ARVN Regiment in a search-and-clear operation in III Corps' area. On 11 November, the Vietnamese marines fought an intensive engagement with a Viet Cong force west of My Tho, which resulted in 19 confirmed enemy dead at a cost of 6 marines killed and 21 wounded. While praising the Vietnamese marines, Captain McWilliams noted that the engagement was not typical. "More often than not," he observed, "the highly mobile Viet Cong could elude the larger, more cumbersome government units." In fact, the Communists only fought if they enjoyed the advantage and an engagement held the promise of victory. Such an instance occurred in early December when Vietnamese marines operating in the western part of Tay Ninh Province in III Corps' area suffered heavy casualties after becoming ensnared in a well-planned and well-executed Viet Cong ambush.

In mid-December, Lieutenant Colonel Khang was relieved as the Commandant of the Vietnamese marines. Although he had not participated in the November coup, he was a Diem political appointee and was viewed as a potential threat by the government's new leaders. To remove this potential problem, Khang was promoted to full colonel and assigned as the RVN military attaché to the Philippines. As the year inched toward its close, a general malaise gripped the country and it did not take long to infect the Vietnamese marines. Lieutenant Colonel Noren, the senior Marine advisor, saw a precipitous drop in morale, and desertion rates were high in nearly every battalion.

In the aftermath of the November coup that claimed the lives of President Diem and his brother, the government entered a period of political instability and uncertainty. Major General Duong Van Minh led the country for less than three months. In January 1964, he was ousted in a bloodless coup by the newly appointed I Corps commander, General Nguyen Khanh, who would only retain the reins of the unstable government for one year. Many senior officers, who had only been in their positions for three months, were replaced by officers loyal to General Khanh. Uncertainty and inaction gripped the government and the military. The situation was ripe for exploitation by Communist forces, and they took advantage of the opportunity.

The North Vietnamese, with complete disregard for the 1962 Geneva Agreement, continued to infiltrate troops and equipment through Laos and into South Vietnam. While this was significant, the most important change as 1963 ended and 1964 began was in the strategy employed by the Viet Cong. The Khanh government had assumed that the Viet Cong would attempt to capitalize on the government's disorganization and inaction by attempting to consolidate their control of the country's populated rural areas. Khanh and his supporters were mistaken in this assumption. The Communist political machine and its military forces had been growing in size and sophistication. By the end of 1963, they were able to muster units of regimental strength and engage like-size South Vietnamese units and defeat them.

The Viet Cong leadership decided that the time was ripe to transition to phase III of Mao Tse-tung's three-phase guerrilla war template and go over to a "general counter-offensive." In a series of violent and successful attacks in II Corps' coastal Binh Dinh Province, two Communist main force regiments quickly reduced the government's presence to the provincial capital and a few district towns. In III Corps, similar attacks threatened to eliminate the government's pacification program. In January 1964, the Viet Cong in the Mekong Delta decisively defeated a multibattalion ARVN heliborne force. In the north, each successive Marine helicopter assault appeared to meet more determined resistance. The Communists had wrested the initiative from the moribund, rudderless South Vietnamese government and were on the offensive.

In contrast, government actions following Diem's assassination were characterized by confusion and indecision. The

Commandant of the Marine Corps Gen Wallace M. Greene Jr. inspects an honor guard of Vietnamese marines at the Cuu Long Navy Yard. To his right is MajGen Richard C. Weede, the USMACV chief of staff.

Strategic Hamlet Program—a major Diem initiative launched in 1961—was abandoned. Diem had begun the program, which was administered by his brother, to provide social and economic programs and security to the country's thousands of rural hamlets. Other than the resettlement of many rural hamlets into government-constructed compounds—often resisted by the villagers being resettled—the program had provided little benefit to the people it was intended to help. Other pacification efforts would soon replace it. As 1963 ended, the overall effectiveness of the South Vietnamese war effort was at its lowest level since the intensification of the U.S. assistance programs in early 1962.

U.S. Military Support Increases

In 1963, the military plans put forward by Secretary of Defense McNamara called for the withdrawal of 1,000 men in January 1964. This number included the 47-man security platoon guarding the Marine aviation task element's compound at Da Nang. The plans further called for withdrawal

of all direct support at some point in the future. In the weeks following President Diem's overthrow and assassination, it became increasingly apparent that these plans were at odds with the facts on the ground. As the war continued in 1964 and the Communist forces strengthened and became more aggressive, the United States reassessed the situation and decided to substantially increase its stake.

In March 1964, President Lyndon B. Johnson, who assumed office upon the assassination of President Kennedy on 22 November 1963, ordered a review of the decisions to withdraw U.S. military personnel and scale back the assistance programs. Secretary McNamara offered several recommendations, including a proposal to support the expansion of the Vietnamese military and paramilitary forces by 50,000 men. The president approved these recommendations, setting the stage for increases in U.S. advisors and assistance. He also ordered key changes to the senior U.S. leadership in South Vietnam. On 22 June 1964, Army General William C. Westmoreland, who had been serving as the USMACV deputy commander, relieved General Harkins as commander of USMACV. The following day, the president announced that General Maxwell D. Taylor, USA, who was then serving as the chairman of the Joint Chiefs, would replace Henry Cabot Lodge as the U.S. ambassador in Saigon.

In one of his first actions as USMACV commander, General Westmoreland requested an increase of an additional 5,100 U.S. military personnel for his command; 900 would serve as advisors, and 4,200 would be support personnel. McNamara discussed this request with the members of the JCS, who agreed to it. The request was forwarded to the president, who approved it in early August. Furthermore, in response to one actual and one alleged North Vietnamese torpedo boat attack on U.S. Navy ships in the Gulf of Tonkin, Congress unanimously passed a resolution on 6 August 1964, authorizing the president "to use all measures, including the commitment of armed forces, to assist [South Vietnam] in the defense of its territorial integrity." Signed by President Johnson five days after its passage, it confirmed, without qualification, the U.S. commitment to the defense of South Vietnam.

A New Crop of VNMC Advisors

In the early weeks of 1964, the 6,109-man Vietnamese Marine Brigade continued its downward spiral. Changes in command at nearly every level, combined with an ever-climbing desertion rate, continued to have a deleterious effect on the brigade's combat readiness. In an attempt to restore the brigade's spirit and combat effectiveness, the Saigon government brought Colonel Le Nguyen Khang back from the Philippines in February, promoted him to brigadier general, and reinstated him as the brigade commandant. With his inspiring leadership and focus on the Vietnamese marines and their dependents, now-General Khang slowly turned the morale and desertion rates around.

During January 1964, General Wallace M. Greene Jr., who had become the Marine Corps' 23d Commandant on New Years Day, made a three-day visit to South Vietnam. After his arrival at Tan Son Nhut Airport, General Greene visited the Cuu Long Navy Yard on the outskirts of Saigon where he inspected an honor guard of Vietnamese marines and received briefings on the operational and political situation. The CMC was accompanied on this visit by Major

General Richard G. Weede, the USMACV chief of staff. His itinerary in the southern part of the country then took him to the III Corps' Mekong Delta, where he visited Cantho and Ca Mau. Flying north, Greene made a short visit to the II Corps' headquarters at Pleiku in South Vietnam's Central Highlands. He then continued on to I Corps for visits at Da Nang and Hue–Phu Bai.

In Da Nang, the CMC toured Shufly facilities and met with several of the enlisted Marines in the unit's mess hall. He awarded 15 Air Medals to Marine Medium Helicopter Squadron 361 (HMM-361) pilots and crewmen and received briefings from Colonel Andre D. Gomez, the subunit's commanding officer. Accompanied by Colonel Gomez, General Greene also attended briefings hosted by the I Corps commander, General Nguyen Khanh, at the general's villa on the outskirts of Da Nang. As noted previously, less than three weeks after this visit, General Khanh, then 36 years old, staged a bloodless coup and became South Vietnam's prime minister.

Throughout the year, the Vietnamese Marine Brigade continued to serve as a major element in the general reserve force. Almost without exception, at least one marine battalion remained in close proximity to Saigon, ready to react to threats in the surrounding area. The remainder of the brigade normally operated nearby, often in support of the government's new "Hop Tac" pacification campaign that had replaced the Strategic Hamlet Program of President Diem. When employed away from Saigon for combat operations, individual VNMC battalions were frequently attached to an ARVN division or a provincial or a corps headquarters. On occasion, the brigade was employed as a multibattalion task force with its brigade headquarters commanding the operation. Unfortunately, these operations were not models of military operational efficiency.

One such operation took place in early January 1964, when two Vietnamese marine battalions and a task force headquarters deployed to Go Cong and Long An Provinces southwest of Saigon to "reestablish government control over the region through systematic small unit operations designed to deny the enemy his usual freedom of movement." Basically a pacification effort, the operation continued until the middle of September, during which the brigade's forces fought not a single major engagement. The senior U.S. Marine advisors later spoke poorly of the conduct of this nine-month operation. Colonel Noren (promoted from lieutenant colonel on 1 July) noted that the brigade's operations "were characterized by inadequate coordination of military and intelligence reporting . . . [and] too little operational activity." His successor, Colonel William P. Nesbit, who assumed duties as the senior Marine advisor on 4 September 1964, remarked that "the capacity of the task force headquarters in staff functioning was marginal."

Two similar, but much shorter, multibattalion operations were undertaken in the early months of 1965. One was conducted in Tay Ninh Province northwest of Saigon and the other in South Vietnam's southernmost province of An Xuyen. Both enjoyed limited success, but failed to significantly reduce the Viet Cong's influence or activities in the provinces.

In mid-1964, the brigade was again expanded and restructured, most significantly with the addition of a fifth infantry battalion. Garrisoned in a small camp about 12 miles north of Saigon, the battalion took 12 months to fill its ranks and complete its training and was not declared combat ready until June 1965.

Brigade restructuring was focused in three areas. The artillery battalion's two 75mm pack-howitzer batteries were combined into a single eight-gun battery and the 105mm howitzer battery was split into two six-howitzer batteries. The training company was deleted from the T/O of the Amphibious Support Battalion and a stand-alone Training Center was established at Thu Duc. Finally, the Brigade Headquarters was reduced in size, and a Task Force Headquarters with two like elements—a Task Force A and a Task Force B—was established.

The U.S. Marine Advisory Division began 1964 with an authorized strength of 11 officers and 9 enlisted men. Before year's end, it would experience a significant increase in its numbers. Concurrent with the dissolution of the MAAG and the restructuring of USMACV, the division was renamed the Marine Advisory Unit, Vietnam, in mid-May. In November, the unit received a T/O increase of one captain and eight first lieutenants. With this increase, Colonel Nesbit assigned one captain and one first lieutenant to the new 5th Infantry Battalion, four first lieutenants to the four other infantry battalions, and two of the remaining first lieutenants as advisors to the motor transport and communications companies. Earlier

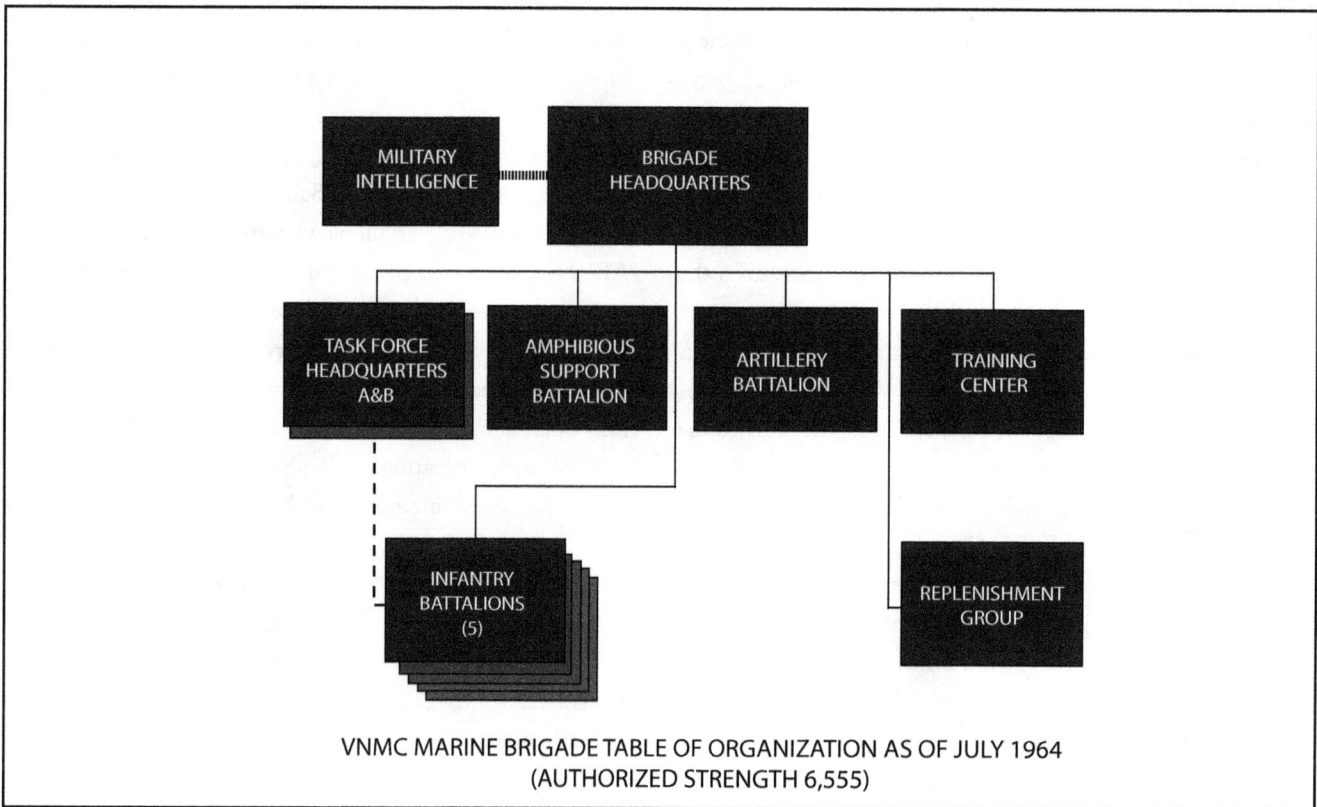

VNMC MARINE BRIGADE TABLE OF ORGANIZATION AS OF JULY 1964
(AUTHORIZED STRENGTH 6,555)

Official U.S. Marine Corps photo

A medic treats a wounded Vietnamese marine during a village sweep operation.

in the year, Colonel Earl E. Anderson, the MAAG chief of staff, directed that the assistant senior Marine advisor be relieved of his additional duties as the artillery battalion advisor. Colonel Noren assigned a captain as the artillery battalion advisor and the remaining first lieutenant as the assistant artillery battalion advisor. By year's end, the Marine Advisory Unit's T/O had expanded to 18 officers (whose military occupational specialties matched their duties) and 6 enlisted Marines.

As 1964 drew to a close, the Vietnamese Marine Brigade could point to several major improvements. It had expanded, had restructured, and was better organized to conduct combat operations. It had acquired new pieces of motor transport equipment and had made the supply system more manageable and responsive. The training center at Thu Duc had graduated 1,464 recruits. More than 700 Vietnamese marine officers and noncommissioned officers had attended training courses in South Vietnam; 42 officers had attended formal schools in the United States; and 52 had undergone training with Marine organizations on Okinawa. Sadly, these improvements would be overshadowed by devastating losses suffered by the VNMC on the last day of the year.

In early December, the South Vietnamese 4th Marine Battalion was assigned duties as the reserve force for the III Corps Tactical Zone (III Corps) located north of Saigon. On 27 December, a Viet Cong force of battalion size overran the town of Binh Gia in III Corps' Phuoc Thy Province, only 35 miles east of Saigon. III Corps officials responded by ordering the 4th Marine Battalion and an elite ARVN Ranger battalion to the area. On 30 December, the battalion, with its two U.S. Marine advisors and three OJT Program participants from 3d MarDiv, recaptured the town, encountering no enemy opposition in the process. Later in the day, an aerial observer spotted a large enemy force approximately two miles west of Binh Gia. A U.S. Army helicopter gunship, responding to a request for an air strike, attacked the enemy force, but it was shot down in the ensuing action, resulting in the loss of its crew.

The 4th Marine Battalion commander, against the advice of Captain Franklin P. Eller, the senior U.S. Marine advisor, ordered one of his companies to secure the crash site and recover the bodies of the dead crewmen. Captain Eller, accompanied by First Lieutenant James P. Kelliher and Staff Sergeant Clifford J. Beaver, both from the OJT Program, chose to move with the relief company. On the morning of 31 December, the company set out for the crash site. Upon reaching the downed helicopter gunship, the company was ambushed by a large Viet Cong force employing .50-caliber machine guns, 57mm recoilless rifles, and 82mm mortars. With intense fire precluding any efforts to maneuver against the superior enemy force, the company called for assistance and began to withdraw to Binh Gia in small groups. Responding to the call for assistance, the battalion commander, along with First Lieutenant Philip O. Brady, the assistant Marine advisor, and Captain Donald G. Cook, the third OJT Marine, moved the remaining three companies of the battalion westward in an attempt to engage the enemy force. While moving through an abandoned rubber plantation, the Vietnamese marines were savagely attacked by an enemy force estimated to number between 1,200 and 1,800 men. By late afternoon, the battalion commander and 28 of his 35 officers were dead. The Marine advisors rallied the remnants of the battalion into small groups and, slipping past Viet Cong units, moved them back to Binh Gia.

During the last days of 1964, the Vietnamese marines suffered their worst defeat of the war. The 326-man battalion saw 112 men killed, 71 wounded, and 13 missing. Nearly 150 weapons and more than a dozen radios were also lost. All of the U.S. Marines who had participated in the action were wounded, and Captain Cook was missing in action. Subsequent to the action, it was learned that the 4th Battalion had been engaged by two main force regiments of the *9th Viet Cong Division*—the first Communist division to become operational in the war. The ARVN Ranger battalion that had been operating close by fared no better. In a violent and well-orchestrated Viet Cong ambush, it suffered nearly 400 casualties.

For the Vietnamese Marine Brigade, in particular, and South Vietnam, in general, 1964 ended on a very sour note. The Viet Cong had demonstrated that they were now capable of operating at the regimental level and were driving the pace of the war. Further, it was becoming clear that the force was transitioning into phase III of Mao's template for protracted war: the successful employment of organized combat forces on battalion, regiment, and division levels against like-size South Vietnamese units. It appeared that no matter how fast the South Vietnam government organized and deployed

forces, and no matter how many pacification programs it initiated, the Communists were always one full step ahead. The same can be said for U.S. assistance and advisory efforts. Their contributions were not keeping pace with what the Viet Cong were employing on the battlefield. In light of these facts, in the last half of 1964 the Johnson administration revisited its commitment to South Vietnam and made plans to increase its efforts.

The OJT Program Continues

The 3d MarDiv and the 1st MAW continued to support the OJT Program in 1963 and 1964, sending company grade officers and staff noncommissioned officers to South Vietnam for 30-day assignments, mainly with ARVN or VNMC units. As the war intensified in 1963, the risks associated with advising or observing Vietnamese combat units increased. Although no Marines were killed while advising the VNMC's battalions in 1963, four Marines were wounded in action; two were members of the permanent Marine Advisory Division, and the other two were 3d MarDiv Marines participating in the OJT Program.

After completing their assignments in South Vietnam, the OJT Program participants drafted after action reports chronicling their experiences and observations. These reports were forwarded to FMFPac where they were made enclosures to an FMFPac letter that was distributed to the CMC; Marine Corps Schools, Quantico, Virginia; FMFLant; and all major Marine Corps commands in the Pacific. The reports for March 1964 were typical and reflected the observations and opinions of program participants. The March cohort of company grade officers included two rifle company commanders, one tank company commander, two company executive officers (one rifle and one tank), one engineer battalion assistant operations officer, one aircraft squadron intelligence officer, and one qualified UH-34D pilot. Their assignments in South Vietnam were equally varied; for example, two served at the company level with VNMC companies, and two served at the company level with ARVN companies, while the UH-34D pilot spent his month in-country flying combat missions out of the Da Nang airfield with Shufly squadron HMM-364.

Although assigned to different units, the officers' observations were often similar and almost universally negative. They frequently cited the lack of discipline of the ARVN soldiers, who often fired their weapons indiscriminately. When night operations were conducted—which was not very often—little noise or light discipline was observed. Two of the American officers—one with a VNMC battalion—cited the improper treatment of prisoners. Interrogation techniques were "brutal," and prisoners were routinely tortured. Materials taken from prisoners were not retained for their intelligence potential, but rather were shared among the soldiers. Two officers—one with a VNMC company—commented that small unit leaders were weak and not aggressive. The officer with the VNMC company further noted that "individual small arms and equipment are poorly maintained" and that the physical fitness of the individual Vietnamese marine was substandard. More than one Marine observer noted the lack of empathy and support shown by the military for the villagers where they were operating. To note that the Vietnamese units did not take advantage of opportunities for civic action would be an understatement.

Significantly, two participants in the OJT Program noted what they believed were serious disconnects between the U.S. advisors and their Vietnamese counterparts. A U.S. Marine captain assigned to a VNMC battalion reported that he "observed resentment towards advisors below the senior Marine advisory level." Another officer, assigned to an ARVN battalion, noted a "lack of communication" between the advisor and the unit commander, particularly when engaged with enemy forces. He said that on many occasions the advisor had no idea what was going on. These observers recommended language training and the need for more experience for U.S. officers before they assumed advisory duties.

These comments stand in stark contrast to the observations made by another Marine captain who was assigned to the 1st Company, 4th Battalion, of the VNMC. He stated that "the individual [Vietnamese] Marine is a tough and fearless leader." Furthermore, he noted that the officers were "excellent," and he spoke positively about their map reading skills (they always knew where they were on the map) and their ability to read a compass. Clearly, it appears that some South Vietnamese units were better—and better led—than others.

In addition to commenting on the performance of the Vietnamese units they were observing, some OJT Program participants offered comments on individual items of clothing and equipment. A Marine captain, a company commander in the 3d Marine Regiment on Okinawa, noted that the U.S. jungle boots issued to him were "outstanding." They dried quickly and permitted good air circulation. He was, however, not enamored with the packs then being issued to U.S. Marines—the same style worn by those who assaulted Okinawa in 1945. He stated that "the U.S. Army haversack utilized by the Vietnamese Marines is far superior to our own in all respects." A Marine captain, a company commander in the 3d Tank Battalion who was assigned to a VNMC infantry company, recommended that "the U.S. Marine Corps adopts [sic] the lightweight camouflage utility uniform worn by the Viet Namese [sic] Marines. This uniform will dry in 15 minutes, is comfortable in hot weather, and is easy to maintain."

Late in 1964, the OJT Program was expanded to include members of Marine commands located in Hawaii. While they continued to be assigned to ARVN units as well as VNMC units, program participants as a rule were assigned to VNMC units that had a permanent U.S. Marine advisor. While they did provide some additional support, their presence was not always viewed as beneficial. One permanent Marine Advisory Division advisor noted that "OJTs were a mixed blessing—they provided some help but they also were an added responsibility for the VNMC commander who was charged with their safety." And their safety could not always be assured. As recounted earlier, in a major operation on 31 December 1964, during which the VNMC's 4th Battalion was dealt a devastating blow by a superior Viet Cong force, OJT Program participants Lieutenant Kelliher and Staff Sergeant Beaver were wounded, and Captain Cook was reported as missing in action. The program continued into 1965 and did not end until major units of the 3d MarDiv landed at Da Nang in March 1965.

A program similar to the OJT Program was started in the second half of 1963 for field grade officers. The Job Related Orientation Program ran for eight days and afforded field grade staff officers from FMFPac commands the opportunity to visit the major U.S. headquarters in South Vietnam and Thailand. In Da Nang, the visiting officers were briefed by the Shufly helicopter task element commander and given orientation flights over the I Corps area. In Saigon, where they were hosted by the senior Marine advisor, they were briefed by USMACV officers and visited with VNMC units

The flight line of HMM-162 in front of the squadron's main hanger in Da Nang is shown in the summer of 1963.

for discussions of tactics and problem areas. After four days in South Vietnam, the officers were flown to Bangkok, where they spent the final four days of their visit. In written reports prepared by officers after their visits, several took the opportunity to provide opinions on the war that went beyond the normal issues of tactics, intelligence, operations, and logistics. Colonel Warren P. Baker, a member of the 3d MarDiv staff, noted that the field advisors with ARVN and VNMC operational units expressed less optimism about the progress of the war than did USMACV staff members. Lieutenant Colonel Harry E. Dickinson stated without qualification that "the commitment of sizeable U.S. combat units should not be effected except to protect the seat of government" and that "as combat units were increased, the forces of Vietnam would do less and less." He concluded by stating, "I strongly disagree that any two or three U.S. divisions could achieve real victory as has been stated in the press."

Shufly Operations: 1963–64

On 6 November 1962, the Shufly task unit was redesignated TE 79.3.3.6. On the same day, Lieutenant Colonel Alton W. McCully, the subunit's executive officer, assumed command. Colonel Ireland, the previous task element commander, returned to Okinawa and assumed command of MAG-16. As previously noted, HMM-162, commanded by Colonel Leu, had relieved Colonel Rathbun's HMM-163 on 12 January

1963. Following on the heels of the squadron's change of command, Lieutenant Colonel George H. Linnemeier, the recipient of four Distinguished Flying Crosses for action in World War II and the Korean War, arrived on 16 January to take command of the MABS-16 subunit from Colonel Davis. Finally, on 29 January, Lieutenant Colonel Harold F. Brown, who had piloted scout–dive bombers during World War II, relieved Colonel McCully as the task element commander.

Flight Operations Continue

Although the monsoon season (October to April in the I Corps area) frequently hampered helicopter operations, HMM-162 flight crews went right to work after relieving HMM-163. On 19 January, the squadron participated in its first operation with an 18-aircraft lift of 300 troops from 2d ARVN Division into a mountainous area 15 miles west of Da Nang. During this mission, the Marine helicopter crews encountered what would be a continuing and troublesome Viet Cong tactic: implanting bamboo stakes in landing zones to impale the helicopters as they landed. In spite of this new hazard, and the fact that two helicopters were struck by small-arms fire while approaching their landing zone, the mission was completed successfully.

Concealed tree stumps also proved hazardous to helicopters during their descents into landing zones in the heavily forested areas of I Corps. On 18 February, while attempting

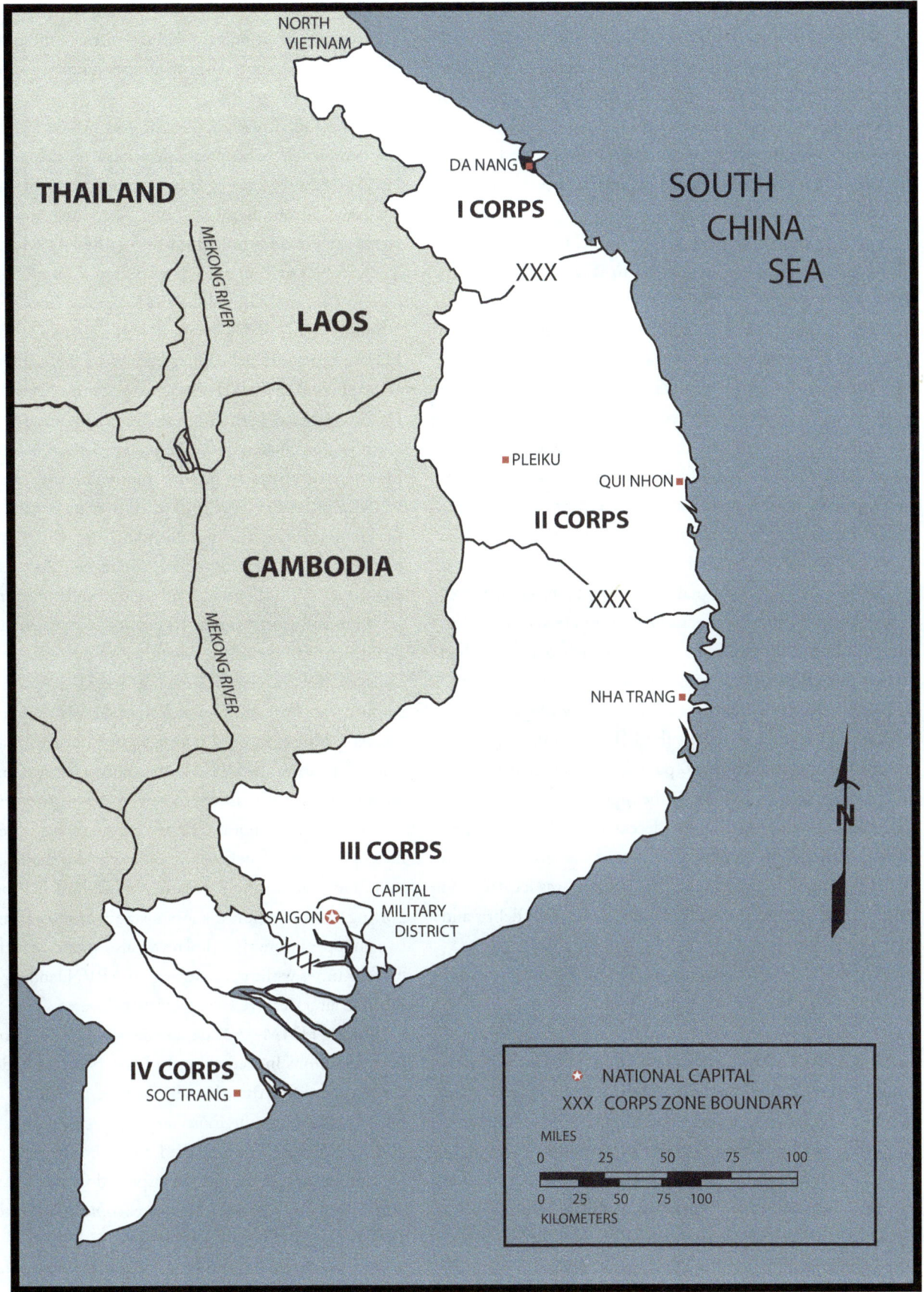

Corps Tactical Zones 1963–1964

THAILAND

NORTH VIETNAM

LAOS

MEKONG RIVER

DA NANG

I CORPS

SOUTH CHINA SEA

XXX

PLEIKU

QUI NHON

II CORPS

CAMBODIA

MEKONG RIVER

XXX

NHA TRANG

III CORPS

N

CAPITAL MILITARY DISTRICT

SAIGON

XXX

IV CORPS

SOC TRANG

★ NATIONAL CAPITAL

XXX CORPS ZONE BOUNDARY

MILES

0   25   50   75   100

0   25   50   75   100

KILOMETERS

to insert troops of the 1st ARVN Division into landing zones about 18 miles southwest of Hue, five helicopters sustained punctures in the bottoms of their fuselages from stumps in the landing zones. Extensive damage sustained by one aircraft required that it be left overnight. Mechanics were flown in the following day to repair the helicopter, which was then flown back to Da Nang.

During the second week of March, HMM-162 lost two UH-34D aircraft while attempting to locate a downed U.S. Army Grumman OV-1 Mohawk (a twin-engine, turboprop, electronic reconnaissance aircraft) and its pilot, who had parachuted into dense jungle at an altitude near 5,000 feet. The combination of the altitude and the high temperature, both of which adversely affected the helicopter's lift capability, made the rescue effort extremely hazardous. Nonetheless, HMM-162 took the mission without hesitation. While employing its hoist to lower an ARVN ranger to the site, the first rescue helicopter crashed when it lost power. Although the crew managed to climb from the wreckage before it caught fire, the copilot, Captain David N. Webster, sustained severe burns in the subsequent explosion. He succumbed to his injuries during the night. A second helicopter that had joined the rescue effort from Da Nang also lost power at the high altitude and crashed in the vicinity of the downed Mohawk. The following day, a third UH-34D that had been stripped of approximately 700 pounds of equipment to allow it to more efficiently operate at the high altitude successfully extracted all survivors and the deceased copilot. The Army pilot, who had been found by the crew of the second downed helicopter, was also evacuated. The Mohawk was located, and Army technicians were helilifted in to examine the debris and evacuate its sensitive electronics equipment.

On 13 March, while shuttling South Vietnamese rangers to Mang Buc (a government outpost southwest of Quang Ngai in northern II Corps), the helicopter came under fire from Viet Cong who had filtered into positions near the rangers' perimeter. Three helicopters employed their door-mounted M60 machine guns to lay down suppressive fire, while the remaining UH-34Ds completed the extraction of the troops in the landing zones. This marked the first recorded instance of a Marine helicopter providing close air support during actual combat. While similar troop lifts were conducted during the first months of HMM-162's deployment, its principal missions—driven in large measure by restrictions imposed by the monsoon rains—were resupply and medical evacuations.

As extended periods of clear weather returned in April, the tempo of helicopter operations quickened with the HMM-162 crews flying more missions into the mountainous areas surrounding Da Nang. Viet Cong opposition also increased. On 13 April, HMM-162 lifted 435 men from the 2d ARVN Division into a suspected Communist stronghold in the mountains along the Song Thu Bon (river) about 30 miles south of Da Nang. For the first time in the war, Marine transport helicopters received a helicopter gunship escort. Five Bell UH-1B Iroquois[*] gunships from the Army's Da Nang–based 68th Aviation Company, armed with M60 machine gun clusters and 2.75-inch rockets, accompanied the Marine helicopters to provide suppressive fire. In addition, VNAF fighter-bombers conducted preparatory air strikes on the landing zones. The initial landing met with no resistance; however, on a return flight to evacuate wounded ARVN soldiers, one UH-34D was hit by eight rounds of enemy small-arms fire and forced down. Its copilot, First Lieutenant John D. Olmen, was wounded. Two other Marine aircraft managed to evacuate Lieutenant Olmen, a wounded American advisor, and one dead and four wounded ARVN soldiers without incident. However, on a return flight to evacuate additional wounded, one of the UH-34Ds sustained heavy damage from enemy fire and was forced down in the vicinity of the first downed helo. Corporal Charley M. Campbell, the downed helicopter's crew chief, was wounded in the thigh, chest, and back. He was quickly evacuated, but a third helicopter supporting the operation a short distance from where the first two choppers were shot down was also shot down after being hit four times while approaching an ARVN landing zone. All downed aircraft were subsequently recovered.

During HMM-162's deployment, Marine helicopter support operations inched closer to Laos. Near the end of April, the Marines lifted three battalions of the 1st ARVN Division's troops into the mountainous areas of western Quang Tri and Thua Thien Provinces near the Laotian border in support of a multiregimental drive against suspected Communist infiltration routes. For 90 days, Marine helicopters flew into and out

---

[*]A single-engine, turbine-powered utility helicopter commonly known as the "Huey."

Major Outposts I Corps and Northern II Corps 1963

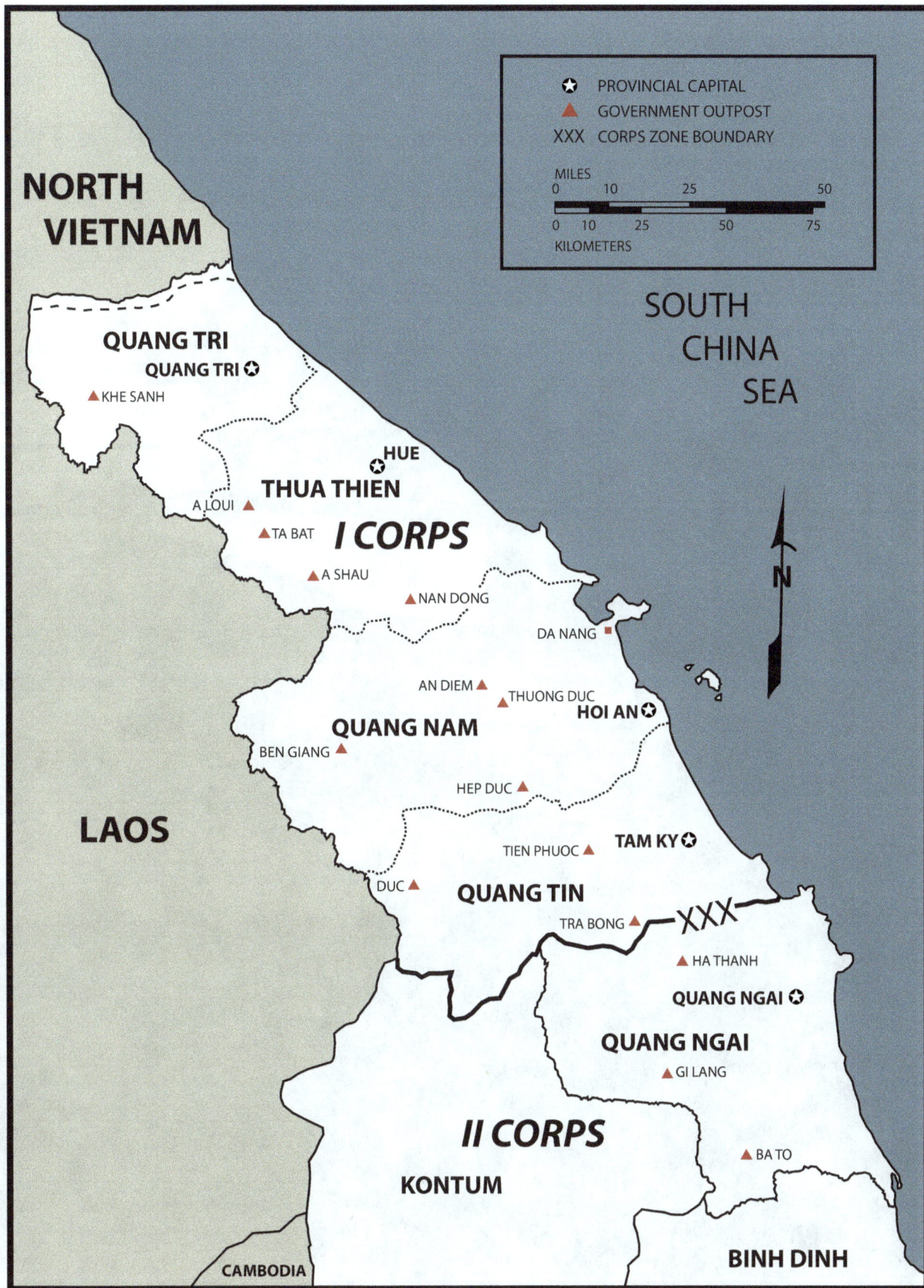

NORTH VIETNAM

SOUTH CHINA SEA

LAOS

CAMBODIA

QUANG TRI
- QUANG TRI ✪
- ▲ KHE SANH

THUA THIEN
- HUE ✪
- A LOUI ▲
- ▲ TA BAT
- *I CORPS*
- ▲ A SHAU
- ▲ NAN DONG

QUANG NAM
- DA NANG ■
- AN DIEM ▲
- ▲ THUONG DUC
- **HOI AN** ✪
- BEN GIANG ▲
- HEP DUC ▲

QUANG TIN
- TIEN PHUOC ▲
- **TAM KY** ✪
- DUC ▲
- TRA BONG ▲ XXX
- ▲ HA THANH

QUANG NGAI
- **QUANG NGAI** ✪
- ▲ GI LANG

II CORPS

KONTUM

BINH DINH

▲ BA TO

Legend
- ✪ PROVINCIAL CAPITAL
- ▲ GOVERNMENT OUTPOST
- XXX CORPS ZONE BOUNDARY

MILES
0 10 25 50

KILOMETERS
0 10 25 50 75

N

Marines of HMM-162, led by LtCol Reinhardt Leu, posed for a group photograph on 28 May 1963. Several of the Marines in the front row had just been awarded Air Medals for combat actions against Viet Cong forces.

Photo courtesy of David H. Hugel

Photo courtesy of David H. Hugel

Three UH-34Ds from LtCol Frank A. Shook's HMM-261 flare into a landing zone to unload their Vietnamese troops during combat operations southwest of Da Nang in the summer of 1963.

of hazardous landing zones at altitudes reaching 4,500 feet. Resupply and medical evacuations comprised the majority of the operations following the initial insertions of troops, but occasionally larger movements were executed to move infantry or artillery units. In a testimony to their proficiency and increasing combat-flying skills, no helicopters were lost, and no Marines were wounded during this extended operation.

In a concurrent operation, one helicopter was lost when 21 of Colonel Leu's aircraft lifted more than 567 troops of the 2d ARVN Division into mountainous zones approximately 22 miles southwest of Tam Ky. On 27 April, one UH-34D was shot down by hostile fire, and its pilot—Captain Virgil R. Hughes—was wounded in the leg. Although the aircraft crash-landed, the remainder of the crew and all embarked ARVN soldiers escaped injury. The helicopter was declared a total loss, making it the first Marine helicopter loss definitely attributable to direct enemy action.

The first week of June saw the return of transports from VMGR-152 and, with them, the Marines from HMM- 261,

the squadron that would replace HMM-162. HMM-162 had flown 17,670 sorties, logging 8,579 hours in the air. The Cessna O-1B Bird Dogs* added approximately 400 sorties and 1,000 hours to these figures. On the other side of the ledger, the squadron had suffered one Marine killed and three wounded, and it had lost three aircraft during its deployment. These figures were testimony to the increased tempo of ARVN operations; the increased activity of the Viet Cong; and, significantly, the increased danger attached to conducting combat "support" operations for the South Vietnamese military. On 8 June 1963, Lieutenant Colonel Frank A. Shook, the commanding officer of HMM-261, relieved Colonel Leu's HMM-162. He committed his squadron to its first combat mission that same day.

One of the largest troop movements conducted by Marine helicopters in the period prior to America's major involvement in the war occurred in mid-August 1963. During the second

*The Marine OE-1 Bird Dog was redesignated as O-1B in 1962.

Landing zones were often small and not well prepared. Here a Marine UH-34D drops into a small landing zone to resupply a remote ARVN outpost.

week of August, the task element staff under the command of Colonel Andre D. Gomez and other American and I Corps Vietnamese officers began planning for an operation that would be a major retrograde movement of South Vietnamese forces from bases near the Laotian border. The plan, to be executed over three days, called for the movement of approximately 1,300 troops with their artillery and equipment from infiltration routes in western Quang Nam Province along the Laotian border to Thoung Duc, a government-held town 30 miles southwest of Da Nang.

On 15 August, 20 HMM-261 helicopters, 18 conducting troop lifts and 2 serving as replacement and search-and-rescue aircraft, began evacuating 500 ARVN troops from the first landing zone. Vietnamese UH-34s and unarmed U.S. Army UH-1Bs also participated in the evacuation. The first landing zone was located along a streambed approximately five miles from the Laotian border. It was surrounded by steep, jungle-covered ridgelines up to 1,000 feet in altitude and could accommodate only three helicopters at a time. Security

was provided by a 125-man ARVN force that covered the evacuation from the ridgelines until it was completed. The evacuation was executed without incident and completed in four hours. At that point, the security force began marching overland to the second landing zone, from which it would be evacuated.

The second landing zone, also small, was located on a valley floor and was surrounded by hills approximately 500 feet high. From this zone, the remaining ARVN troops, two 105mm howitzers, and the 125-man security force from the first landing zone were evacuated on 16 and 17 August. With very few complications—a concern about possible fuel contamination slowed the operation for a short period—the evacuation was completed on 17 August without serious incident and with no losses. Furthermore, during the three-day operation, not a single aircraft or soldier had been hit by enemy fire.

This three-day movement of 1,300 ARVN troops, with their equipment and supplies, was one of the most successfully executed helicopter operations conducted in South Vietnam in the early 1960s. Its success was attributed to two factors: the detailed planning by all units, particularly the South Vietnamese plans for the ground defense of the landing zones, and the extraordinary coordination between the airborne Air Support Operations Center, the operational aircraft, and the air liaison on the ground. These factors were instrumental in coordinating and overcoming problems in this multiservice, bilingual effort.

In the period following the mid-August retrograde operation, HMM-261's operations continued at a normal level. The squadron lost its second UH-34D to mechanical problems only two weeks before its scheduled departure from South Vietnam. On 16 September, the helicopter crashed 25 miles west-southwest of Hue while carrying a South Vietnamese assault force. The crew and passengers escaped without injury. The aircraft, damaged beyond repair, was stripped of its usable parts and burned.

Shortly after this incident, the first elements of HMM-361 began arriving to replace the departing HMM-261. When HMM-261 ended operations, it had flown 11,406 sorties and accumulated 5,288 combat flying hours. The squadron's UH-34Ds had lifted more than 6,000 troops and nearly 1.9-million pounds of cargo, as well as conducted more than 600 medical evacuations. HMM-361, commanded by Lieutenant Colonel Thomas J. Ross, who had earned five Distinguished Flying Crosses for combat flying in World War II and Korea, relieved Colonel Shook's HMM-261 on 2 October 1963.

Less than a week after assuming operational responsibility, HMM-361 suffered its first combat losses. On 8 October, two UH-34Ds crashed almost simultaneously while on a search-and-rescue mission 38 miles southwest of Da Nang. The crashes cost the lives of the four pilots, five Marine crewmen, the squadron's flight surgeon, and two Navy corpsmen. Contemporary news accounts cited this tragic incident as the greatest loss of American lives in a single event up to that point in the war.

Darkness on 8 October precluded locating the two downed aircraft. By the time they were found on 9 October, Viet Cong forces had surrounded the crash sites and were waiting for the recovery aircraft to arrive. Initial attempts to enter the sites were repulsed by intense ground fire. An ARVN security

Photo courtesy of David H. Hugel

The Shufly Marines' cantonment in Da Nang in the summer of 1963.

Photo courtesy of David H. Hugel

An HMM-261 UH-34D extracts a small ARVN force from a landing zone near Da Nang in South Vietnam's I Corps.

force was requested, and later in the day, 254 South Vietnamese soldiers were lifted into landing zones a short distance from the crash sites. Their mission was to assault the crash sites and clear them of enemy resistance. While inserting the ARVN troops, HMM-361's aircraft were again subjected to intense ground fire and were hit nine times.

The following day, as the ARVN forces closed on the crash sites, three HMM-361 helicopters, supported by

Cpl David H. Hugel, a Shufly combat photographer, stands in front of a Marine GV-1 Hercules transport. The twice-weekly resupply runs made by these aircraft brought mail, spare parts, and small items of equipment to the Marines at Da Nang.

armed helicopter and fixed-wing aircraft, managed to insert an inspection team into the sites to recover the bodies and survey the wreckage. Intense automatic weapons fire forced the UH-34Ds to depart the landing zones, leaving the inspection team to find cover on the ground. After the Communist fire had been suppressed, the HMM-361 helicopters returned and evacuated the inspection team and all of the Marine and Navy casualties. There was some speculation that the two helicopters had collided in flight while attempting to evade enemy ground fire. However, the inspection team found evidence of small-arms fire in the wreckage of the two aircraft. That evidence, plus the positions of the two downed aircraft, led Colonel Ross to believe that the helicopters had been shot down by hostile fire.

On 11 October, a third helicopter was forced down after being hit twice in the engine and once in the wheel strut during an ARVN resupply mission. Once again, South Vietnamese ground forces provided security while mechanics flown in from Da Nang replaced the helicopter's engine. Although the last two weeks of October were characterized by uneventful resupply and medical evacuation missions, October had seen HMM-361's helicopters fired at on 46 different occasions and hit 18 times—a one-month record for Marine helicopter squadron operations in South Vietnam.

With the arrival of torrential monsoon rains in the Da Nang area in mid-November, HMM-361's combat operations would diminish to a low level for the remainder of the year. In December, the squadron flew only 230 sorties for a total of 338 flight hours.

As the new year arrived, resupply and medical evacuations constituted the bread-and-butter missions for HMM-361. However, even these missions were becoming dangerous. On 3 January 1964, the squadron suffered its first loss of the year when a UH-34D on a medical evacuation mission was hit six times during its descent into the landing zone and crashed into the jungle. None of the crew was injured, and all were quickly rescued by a second UH-34D. This downed helicopter marked the second loss definitely attributable to enemy fire since Shufly's arrival in-country nearly two years earlier.

A much more difficult mission was passed to HMM-361 the following week. It involved the evacuation of a 200-man Civilian Irregular Defense Group (CIDG) force and its American advisor from a mountainous area about 30 miles west-southwest of Da Nang. While the force was conducting a reconnaissance mission, adverse weather had allowed a Viet Cong force of undetermined strength to get too close to the CIDG camp and possibly destroy it before the weather improved. With only limited intelligence available, Colonel Ross elected to first conduct aerial reconnaissance in an O-1B Bird Dog. The reconnaissance revealed an extremely poor landing zone—a hilltop knot exposed to a 360-degree field of fire. Switching to a UH-34D and flying the lead helicopter into the zone, the squadron commander's helo took heavy enemy fire, resulting in hits puncturing the aft section of the fuselage and wounding the loadmaster. The second helicopter, following close behind, was also hit. Colonel Ross led the 14 UH-34Ds a safe distance from the landing zone where he and the American CIDG force advisor discussed moving the troops to an adjacent and more secure landing zone. After some delay, the Vietnamese unit moved to the new landing zone and the HMM-361 pilots completed the evacuation without further incident.

With enemy fire on Marine aircraft increasing in frequency, concern began to focus on the issue of administering aid to pilots and crew members wounded in flight. A crew member wounded in the helicopter's cabin could be attended to by anyone else in the cabin. For pilots, however, there was no alternative but to land the aircraft—frequently not possible in the rugged Viet Cong–infested mountainous jungle—then pull the wounded pilot from the cockpit's side window and lower him to the ground. A safer and faster method—bringing the pilot from his seat directly into the aircraft's cabin—was devised by Lance Corporal Larry R. Rich, an innovative Marine crew chief. Rich knew that if the permanent bolts holding the cockpit seats in place were removed, the seat would drop into the cabin. He removed these permanent bolts and replaced them with castellated nuts, inserted cotter

pins in the nuts, and used safety wire to connect the bolt heads. A wounded pilot could now be lowered into the cabin by his crew chief in less than a minute by simply pulling out the cotter pins, unscrewing the castellated nuts, and unfastening the pilot's safety belt. For his innovative thinking, Rich's commanding officer, Colonel Ross, recommended the lance corporal for the Navy Commendation Medal.

As January drew to a close, so too did HMM-361's tour as the Shufly squadron. While the early arrival of the monsoon rains had somewhat limited the squadron's ability to fly combat missions, it had flown 4,236 combat hours and just under 7,000 sorties. Moreover, its officers and enlisted crew members had acquitted themselves in a manner that would make any squadron commander proud. In a February 1964 awards ceremony at Marine Corps Air Station Iwakuni, Japan, Major General Frank C. Tharin, the 1st MAW commanding general, recognized 55 squadron members with awards, remarking, "I'm proud to be a member of the same organization as you men." Four Marines—Captains John W. Alber, Robert K. Ervi, and Paul H. Wagener, and Lance Corporal Phillip B. Adams—were awarded the Purple Heart. In addition, 21 HMM-361 Marines—ranging in grade from corporal to major—were awarded the Air Medal, and 30 enlisted Marines received the combat air crew insignia.

On 1 February, Lieutenant Colonel John H. La Voy, commanding Marine Medium Helicopter Squadron 364 (HMM-364), relieved Colonel Ross. Colonel La Voy was a helicopter combat veteran of the Korean War. Two weeks earlier, Colonel Robert A. Merchant, who had served as an artillery battalion commander in World War II and as a Marine attack squadron commander in Korea, assumed command of the Shufly task element. And on 7 February, Lieutenant Colonel Samuel G. Beal, a veteran of World War II and Korea, relieved Lieutenant Colonel Robert M. Cassidy as the commander of the MABS-16 subunit.

In January 1964, while still the commander of the task element, Colonel Gomez had been advised by USMACV that the entire task element would be withdrawn from RVN during the first half of 1964. Further, prior to the Shufly task element's departure, it would be tasked to establish a program to train VNAF pilots to fly the UH-34Ds and Vietnamese mechanics to maintain them. It was planned that a VNAF squadron would take over the Marines' 24 helicopters on

LCpl Larry R. Rich of HMM-361 demonstrates the procedure he developed for removing a wounded pilot from the seat of his UH-34D helicopter while the aircraft is in flight.

30 June 1964, and the entire task element would return to Okinawa.

As a consequence of these assignments, when his squadron took over from HMM-361 on 1 February, Colonel La Voy found himself a man with many missions. His principal mission was to provide combat support for South Vietnam's ground forces in I Corps. Three additional goals would require his time in the coming months. The first was to train an adequate number of Vietnamese pilots in flying UH-34D helicopters so that they would be capable of assuming the squadron's missions on 30 June. He also had to train South Vietnamese maintenance personnel adequately to ensure the flightworthiness of the aircraft that would soon be theirs. Finally, he had to lay the groundwork for the orderly transfer of 24 UH-34D helicopters and all of the task element's maintenance facilities to the VNAF. While the entire unit pushed hard to accomplish these missions, the burden of responsibility weighed most heavily on Colonel La Voy.

The first class of eight Vietnamese pilots began its 50-hour course of flight instruction on 4 February, which included formation flying, landing practice, and night and instrument flying. Because each student pilot had already qualified as a

South Vietnamese troops unload ammunition from a Marine UH-34D while a loadmaster, standing on top of the wheel and wheel strut, communicates with the pilot.

copilot and had at least 25 hours of flight time in a VNAF UH-34D aircraft, training was conducted concurrently with normal operations. As a result, the Vietnamese pilots, flying as copilots on operational squadron missions, were able to gain firsthand knowledge of the helicopter tactics being employed in the northern provinces by their Marine trainers. The first class of VNAF pilots graduated on 9 March. Subsequent classes would be conducted through 1964 with improved instruction, including flying sections of two and four helicopters as integral elements of larger Marine operations.

While the ground crews were keeping the UH-34Ds in the air, they provided extensive training to Vietnamese mechanics; crew chiefs; and engineering, supply, operations, and ordnance personnel. Although language was a problem

and the training mission meant a considerable increase in the workload for these already busy maintenance crews, the requisite knowledge and skills were successfully transferred to their Vietnamese students.

The monsoon rains severely limited flight operations through March, but brief periods of clearing did allow HMM-364 to conduct limited operational missions. On 5 March, with support from U.S. Army and VNAF helicopters, the squadron lifted an ARVN patrol from its base at An Diem to a landing zone adjacent to the Laotian border. When an operational accident forced an Army Huey gunship down en route, two Marine helicopters quickly rescued the crew and the helicopter's weapons, while plans were made to recover the downed helicopter. In the afternoon, the Marines returned with 15 helicopters, a 64-man ARVN security team, 2 Army U-1Bs, and a maintenance crew. The maintenance team quickly repaired the downed helicopter, which was then flown back to Da Nang.

To improve the safety and efficiency of helicopter operations, La Voy's crews made equipment and operational changes based on their experiences. To increase protection to the helicopter's port side, the squadron's metalsmiths developed and built a flexible mount for an additional M60 machine gun. This improvement called for an additional crew member, which lowered the carrying capacity of the aircraft, but allowed a gunner to fire at targets on the left side of the aircraft. After testing proved the concept to be sound, all 24 helicopters were fitted with a second M60 machine gun.

Prior to HMM-364's arrival, loadmaster duties had been rotated among many of the squadron's Marines. To improve the efficiency of loading helicopters—a critical consideration when landing in zones at high altitudes or under enemy fire—Colonel La Voy assigned one pilot and two crew chiefs to permanent loadmaster duties. While a relatively minor fix, it improved the coordination of the Marines' helicopter operations and ARVN ground forces.

April saw the return of good weather and, with it, the resumption of ARVN offensives into the rugged mountains surrounding Da Nang. On 6 April, the squadron participated in an allied helicopter lift carrying 42 ARVN soldiers from Tam Ky to a landing zone about 18 miles directly west of Quang Ngai. The mission was executed without incident. However, operations on 14 April to evacuate wounded ARVN infantrymen from a hillside landing zone on the Laotian border resulted in the squadron's first helicopter loss. While leaving the landing zone under enemy fire, a UH-34D was hit in the engine and plunged 150 feet down a hillside, crashing through the jungle and into a stream. Fortunately, the only injury was a broken leg suffered by the crew chief. The crew and passengers carried the injured Marine up the hill to the ARVN landing zone where they were evacuated without further incident.

In late April, HMM-364 joined with VNAF and U.S. Army helicopters to support a multibattalion ARVN offensive into a mountainous Viet Cong stronghold located along the northern border of II Corps. Code-named Operation Sure Wind 202, it required all of the transport helicopter assets available in I and II Corps. HMM-364's mission was to lift a 420-man ARVN battalion from the airfield at Quang Ngai to a landing zone approximately 30 miles to the west. Although the landing zone was prepared by 12 Vietnamese Skyraiders and 5 U.S. Army Huey gunships, the Viet Cong's .50- and .30-caliber machine-gun fire was so intense around the landing zone that all aircraft were ordered back to Quang Ngai to refuel and rearm. The second attempt to land met with more success, but it was not without cost. The first UH-34Ds touched down at 1230, and several immediately sustained hits from automatic weapons fire. One aircraft, hit during its descent and critically damaged, crashed in the zone. The crew was quickly picked up by a search-and-rescue helicopter piloted by Major John R. Braddon. The second troop lift entered the zone at approximately 1355, and several Marine and one VNAF helicopters were hit by enemy .50-caliber machine-gun fire. The VNAF aircraft lost its tail rotor controls and crashed in the zone, where the crew was quickly picked up by Major Braddon's aircraft. When the fourth and final lift of the day was executed at 1730, 374 of the 420-man battalion had been lifted into the zone. Of the 19 participating Marine helicopters, 15 had been hit, and only 11 of the Marine and VNAF helicopters assigned to the operation remained airworthy. Fourteen Marine helicopters, many of which were repaired during the night, completed the lift the following morning.

The USMACV and II Corps staffs had originally planned to employ the Marine helicopters only for the assault phase of the operation. However, in light of the enemy resistance and the anticipated ARVN requirements in the days ahead, the American command in Saigon directed the Shufly Marines to support Sure Wind 202 for its duration. When the operation concluded on 25 May, HMM-364's crews had flown 983 sorties for a total of 800 combat flight hours.

On 1 June, HMM-364 helicopters returned to II Corps to support Operation Sure Wind 303. In two days of flying, 15 UH-34Ds contributed 180 sorties to the assault phase of the operation. Unlike Sure Wind 202, the missions were executed without incident, and no battle damage was sustained by the Marine aircraft.

Orders Extend and Expand Shufly's Mission

Increased Viet Cong activity and the limited ability of the

ARVN forces to respond unassisted to enemy attacks had led senior USMACV planners in late May 1964 to conclude that U.S. advisors and combat support forces would be needed for the foreseeable future. As a key component of these combat support forces, the Shufly element in Da Nang was about to receive a change in orders. General Westmoreland proposed to the CinCPac that the Marine helicopter squadron and its supporting organizations be retained at Da Nang indefinitely. He further recommended that HMM-364 move forward with its plan to turn over its helicopters and maintenance equipment to the VNAF on 30 June as scheduled and that the squadron then be replaced by another, fully equipped Marine UH-34D helicopter squadron. CinCPac concurred and passed the recommendations to the JCS, who approved them on 10 June 1964. The Marine Corps began immediate preparations to deploy another fully equipped medium helicopter squadron to South Vietnam's I Corps.

The Shufly squadron saw its mission again expanded when it was directed to begin supporting the operations of U.S. forces. USMACV directed Marine helicopters to provide search-and-rescue support to U.S. aerial reconnaissance operations that had begun flying over Laos and North Vietnam. After 7 June, at least two UH-34Ds (one section) would be stationed either at Quang Tri or Khe Sanh, ready to conduct search-and-rescue missions in support of U.S. and VNAF pilots. While deployed, the Marine helicopters were also able to provide critically needed support to Marine Detachment, Advisory Team One, located eight miles north of Khe Sanh on Tiger Tooth Mountain (Dong Voi Mep in Vietnamese). At 5,500 feet elevation, this mountain was the highest terrain feature in northern I Corps.

The advisory team provides an interesting insight into one of the several groups of Marines that supported the South Vietnamese government in the years before major combat units were committed in March 1965. The unit, designated the Signal Engineering Survey Unit, consisted of 3 officers and 27 enlisted Marines assigned from FMFPac's 1st Radio Company and Headquarters, Marine Corps. Commanded by future Commandant, then-Major Alfred M. Gray Jr., the unit arrived in Da Nang on 20 May accompanied by a 76-man security detachment from Company G, 2d Battalion, 9th Marines, commanded by First Lieutenant Raymond J. Otlowski. U.S. Air Force Fairchild C-123 Provider transports

lifted the unit and its security detachment to Khe Sanh in the northwest corner of South Vietnam's Quang Tri Province. There it remained while building a supply base and establishing a sizeable force of replacements for the Marines that would deploy to the austere operating base on Tiger Tooth Mountain.

On 13 June, Army UH-1B helicopters successfully lifted Major Gray plus nine enlisted men and several thousand pounds of equipment to a small landing zone that had been cleared by ARVN soldiers near the mountaintop. On this same day, a Marine UH-34D attempting to land with supplies for Major Gray's team was caught in severe downdrafts and crashed. The crew escaped injury, but the aircraft was declared a total loss. Radios and machine guns were removed and the helicopter was burned. Inclement weather then terminated flight operations until 21 June, when Shufly helicopters completed lifting the 73 Marines and approximately 100 ARVN troops to the landing zone. An additional pool of 81 Marines—both security forces and radiomen—remained at Khe Sanh to relieve the Marines on the mountaintop when needed.

Signals intelligence was the unit's mission, and from its mountaintop north of Khe Sanh, the unit "routinely picked up North Vietnamese radio transmissions describing activity up and down the [Ho Chi Minh] Trail." The Marines operated for nearly a month without adverse incident until, during the second week of July, a severe storm struck their mountaintop base, blowing down tents and antennae, destroying fighting positions, and rendering radio operations impossible. On 17 July, a Viet Cong force probed the Marines' lines and initiated a two-hour, intense machine-gun and rifle exchange. Although no Marines were wounded in the firefight, their location had been comprised. The next day, USMACV ordered Major Gray's unit to withdraw. Employing all available helicopters, HMM-162 lifted the 92-man team and its 92,000 pounds of equipment off Tiger Tooth Mountain, depositing them safely at Khe Sanh before the end of the day on 19 July. On 22 July, U.S. Air Force C-123s airlifted them to Da Nang.

On 13 August, Major Gray was relieved by Captain Raymond A. Becker, a communications officer from the 1st Radio Company. Shortly after Becker's arrival, the Company G security detachment from the 9th Marine Regiment

A formation of Marine UH-34Ds transport ARVN troops into the mountains southwest of Da Nang.

was relieved by Company K, 3d Battalion, 3d Marines, commanded by Captain William R. Irwin. Under Captain Becker, Advisory Team One deployed on 19 August with its radiomen and approximately 4,000 pounds of equipment to Dong Bach Ma, a 3,500-foot-high mountain approximately 25 miles northwest of Da Nang. The mountaintop, accessible from Route 1 by a hard surface road, was the site of an abandoned French resort. The team established its operations center in an old but well-preserved religious building. After initial support provided by ARVN trucks helped to establish the communicators and their security detachment, additional support was provided by Shufly helicopters. The

radio operators plied their trade without incident until 10 September 1964, when the unit was returned to Da Nang and disbanded.

Several other Marine units served in South Vietnam in various capacities and at different times in the period before March 1965. A Marine guard detachment provided much needed security for the U.S. embassy in Saigon. In response to increasing threat levels in 1964, its size was increased until only the U.S. embassy in Paris could boast of a larger detachment. By the end of 1964, the Saigon embassy detachment numbered 30 Marines. A special operations group—with 6 officers and 21 enlisted Marines—sharpened its skills in

South Vietnam's counterinsurgency environment while operating under the control of USMACV. Okinawa-based 3d Reconnaissance Battalion Marines undertook an extensive survey of Cam Ranh Bay to ascertain its value as a potential naval port. In late 1964, the Marine Corps was assigned a share of the advisory billets to ARVN units. As a result, 60 officers and noncommissioned officers were assigned to Vietnamese army units in I Corps. Four-man teams—each with a captain, first lieutenant, gunnery sergeant, and corporal (radio operator)—were hastily formed and sent south from the 3d MarDiv on Okinawa. The first of these teams arrived in mid-September.

Also in late 1964, two advisor billets were created for Marines to support the Vietnamese Navy. Marines assigned to these billets supported Vietnamese naval units operating in the Rung Sat Special Zone, a vast mangrove swamp area located southeast of Saigon. This zone straddled the Long Tao River, which was the main commercial shipping channel from the South China Sea to Saigon. Communist insurgents infested this nearly impenetrable area and were posing a serious threat to ships arriving to and departing from Saigon. Thus, by year's end, U.S. Marines were providing advisory support to three of South Vietnam's four military services. Incrementally, but steadily, the Marines were getting into the fight in South Vietnam, a fight that was showing no signs of abating.

To devote itself full-time to preparations for turning its helicopters and equipment over to South Vietnam's air force, Colonel Le Voy's squadron ended combat support operations on 16 June 1964. When this task was completed, the squadron began to depart, with the last of HMM-364's Marines leaving Da Nang for Okinawa on 30 June. VNAF's newly formed 217th Squadron informally accepted HMM-364's helicopters on 19 June. Formal acceptance would come 10 days later, with appropriate dignitaries on hand to bear witness to this significant milestone.

While HMM-364's pilots, crew chiefs, and mechanics were completing training for the Vietnamese squadron that would assume ownership of their helicopters, HMM-162's flight crews were flying their UH-34Ds into the airfield at Da Nang from the USS *Valley Forge*. Lieutenant Colonel Oliver W. Curtis, HMM-162's commanding officer and the recipient of four Distinguished Flying Crosses for service in World

War II and the Korean War, assumed operational responsibility for the Shufly mission on 17 June.

HMM-162's first major troop lift came in early July when the squadron was tasked to helilift urgently needed reinforcements to the Nam Dong CIDG camp in south-central Thua Thien Province. The camp and surrounding Montagnard villages were defended by only a few U.S. Army Special Forces and Australian advisors and three CIDG companies with fewer than 90 men each. On 6 July, Communist forces launched a large ground attack against Nam Dong's barbed wire–enclosed main camp. Shortly after 0400, with the camp holding out against intense mortar and machine-gun fire, Army Captain Roger H. C. Donlon, the Special Forces officer in charge, radioed for assistance. At 0600, six Marine helicopters loaded with Special Forces and South Vietnamese reinforcements, and accompanied by two Army Huey gunships providing cover, departed Da Nang for Nam Dong. Initial attempts to land the reinforcements failed as the mortar and ground fire was too intense. The entire flight returned to Da Nang to refuel. At 0945, air strikes were conducted on the high ground to the south and west of the camp. Then, led by Colonel Curtis, 18 UH-34Ds accompanied by 4 UH-1B gunships began landing a 93-man relief force and evacuating the outpost's dead and wounded. At 1545, a flight of 10 UH-34Ds returned with 9,500 pounds of ammunition, medical supplies, radios, and other equipment. By then, the battle was over and the camp remained in friendly hands. But the cost was considerable: 2 Americans, an Australian advisor, and 55 South Vietnamese soldiers had been killed. Captain Donlon, who would earn the Medal of Honor for this action, and 64 Vietnamese combatants had been wounded. The Viet Cong failed to overrun the camp and left 62 dead in the area surrounding the outpost.

As July wore on, the squadron's daily missions continued. Most were calls for resupply and medical evacuation and were flown in the face of increasing enemy gunfire. On 6 and 8 July, squadron helicopters were hit while flying medical evacuations. On 15 July, a UH-34D was hit by small-arms fire while supporting a routine resupply mission south of Da Nang. And on 9 August, another HMM-162 helicopter drew fire while evacuating a wounded U.S. advisor from a coastal village eight miles west of Tam Ky.

The squadron conducted its last major heliborne assault

mission during the first week of September. Fifteen HMM-162 helicopters combined with Army, Air Force, and VNAF aircraft to support a 2d ARVN Division heliborne assault against Communist infiltration routes in the southwestern border region of Quang Nam Province. No enemy resistance was encountered, and the lift was completed without incident. Support continued through the next morning. When the operation was completed, the Marines had flown 265 sorties for a total of 180.2 flight hours.

Soon the Marine flight crews would have another enemy to fight: the monsoon rains and their accompanying typhoons. The first—Typhoon Violet—struck the second week in September, causing all flights to be cancelled on 14 September. When flights resumed the afternoon of the following day, HMM-162 conducted an emergency evacuation of storm victims from Tam Ky, which had been particularly hard hit. On 21 September, in the face of a more severe storm, Colonel Curtis was ordered to displace his squadron to Nha Trang, some 325 miles to the south. At this more secure location, the squadron harbored from the storm until 23 September when it was safe to return to Da Nang. That storm—Typhoon Tilda—caused considerable damage to the task element's facilities at Da Nang. Most permanent buildings had water damage; electrical power and teletype communications were lost for a week; and only concerted efforts kept power outages at the water point and the mess hall to a minimum. On the day of their return, HMM-162 crews resumed combat operations, flying 19 passengers and 4,000 pounds of cargo to Tien Phuoc, a government town located seven miles west of Tam Ky.

On 8 October 1964, Colonel Curtis passed responsibility for all helicopters and maintenance equipment to Lieutenant Colonel Joseph Koler Jr., commanding officer of HMM-365. In its three-month deployment, HMM-162 had flown approximately 6,600 sorties for a total of just over 4,400 flight hours. Many of the flights had been humanitarian missions to assist citizens in the wake of the typhoons that had ravaged the northern provinces.

Colonel Koler, who had started his Marine career as an infantry platoon leader in China after World War II, lost no time in getting his squadron into action. On its first day of operations, the squadron lifted more than 25,000 pounds of cargo to various camps around Da Nang. The following day,

12 helicopters lifted a force of ARVN troops to an outpost in Quang Nam Province that was less than seven miles from the Laotian border. These initial flights were not executed without some adversity. On 11 October, eight UH-34Ds were fired on by hostile forces as they landed a 112-man ARVN unit 10 miles west-southwest of Tam Ky. The following day, the squadron lost its first aircraft when a UH-34D lost power and crashed while attempting to take off from a landing zone located high in the mountains of Quang Nam Province. Later, while approaching a poorly protected landing zone 10 miles southwest of Tam Ky, the squadron suffered its first casualties when small-arms fire wounded both the copilot and the crew chief. The pilot managed to fly the helicopter to Tam Ky, where the seriously wounded copilot was evacuated and the crew chief was administered first aid.

On 4 November, Typhoon Iris struck the South Vietnamese coast. Except for emergency medical evacuations, the following week of continuous rain, wind, and fog caused all flight operations to be cancelled. On 10 November—the Marine Corps' birthday—flight operations resumed. On that day, HMM-365 flight crews rescued 144 flood victims, employing the helicopters' hoists to pluck many of them from trees and rooftops. The next day, in poor visibility and harassed by small-arms fire that hit three of the squadron's aircraft, the unit lifted an additional 1,136 flood victims to safety. On 16 November, Typhoon Kate arrived, adding more to the misery of the South Vietnamese peasants living in the low flatlands adjacent to the coast. HMM-365 and VNAF helicopter units located in the I Corps area moved quickly to address yet another humanitarian disaster; however, the magnitude of the rescue efforts required as a result of this storm, coming before humanitarian relief had been completed for the previous typhoon's victims, proved to be beyond their capabilities. To support relief efforts, Colonel Curtis's HMM-162—now assigned to the U.S. Seventh Fleet's Special Landing Force—flew his squadron ashore on 17 November and participated in the humanitarian relief effort for the next six days. By 23 November, HMM-162 had flown over 600 hours and conducted 1,020 sorties in support of the disaster relief operations.

In response to heightened threat levels in the Da Nang area, the Shufly security force was significantly increased in November. On 25 November, the 2d Battalion, 9th Marines, security force was relieved by Company L, 3d Battalion, 9th Marines. The company was reinforced with engineers, 81mm mortar teams, and countermortar radar personnel. While Captain John Sheridan, the company commander, retained tactical control of his infantry unit, the overall 255-man organization—designated the Security Detachment, Marine Unit Vietnam—was commanded by Major William F. Alsop, the battalion's executive officer. The reinforced rifle company was split, with one element providing security for the Shufly hangar and flight line while the other took responsibility for the living quarters. The engineers built ammunition bunkers, machine-gun positions, and mortar pits, and Captain Sheridan established a reaction force prepared to board trucks to defend the squadron's aircraft and maintenance facilities against enemy attack.

As 1964 drew to a close, the Marines could count more than 800 of their number in South Vietnam. Most were in I Corps and included the Shufly squadron, with its command and support elements; the 255-man 3d Battalion, 9th Marines Security Detachment; and 60 Marine advisors attached to I Corps ARVN units. U.S. Marine advisors to the VNMC served throughout the country, and a Marine guard detachment provided security for the U.S. embassy in Saigon. Many more were soon to arrive. By the end of 1965, Marines in South Vietnam would dwarf this 800-plus Marine force.

While flying flood-relief missions into December, HMM-365 also continued to support combat operations throughout the I Corps area. The monsoon rains caused the cancellation of many of the planned heliborne operations; nevertheless, the brief periods of good weather allowed the squadron to conduct its resupply and medical evacuation missions, even into the most remote and mountainous regions of I Corps. As of 31 December, the squadron's crews had flown more than 6,700 sorties for a total of 4,700 hours of flight time. And as 1964 drew to a close, Colonel Koler's squadron had passed the midpoint of its deployment. On 31 December, FMFPAC redesignated the Shufly task element. From that date until it was folded into the 9th Marine Expeditionary Brigade (9th MEB) in mid-March 1965, it would be known as Task Unit 79.3.5, Marine Unit Vietnam.

The End of the Beginning: January–March 1965

The devastating losses suffered by South Vietnam's 4th Marine Battalion and ARVN Ranger battalion near the town of Binh Gia in Phuoc Thy Province at year's end were a harbinger of things to come. The Viet Cong's successful multiregiment operation reflected a combat force capable of closing with large ARVN and VNMC units and defeating them. The initiative was now clearly with the Communist forces. General Westmoreland reported the action at Binh Gia as the start of the final Communist offensive. He saw it as "an intensive military challenge which the Vietnamese government could not meet with its own resources."

Westmoreland had more than just the Binh Gia debacle on which to base his observations. Attacks of increasing intensity against American and South Vietnamese forces—Americans in South Vietnam now numbered more than 23,000—had been escalating for some time and continued to grow as the new year approached. For instance, on 1 November 1964, Communist forces mortared U.S. facilities at the Bien Hoa air base near Saigon, killing four American soldiers while destroying five Martin B-57 Canberra bombers and badly damaging eight others. On Christmas Day, insurgents bombed a U.S. officers' quarters in Saigon, killing 2 Americans and wounding over 50 others.

On 7 December, U.S. Marine and Army helicopters airlifted 240 soldiers of the ARVN's 11th Ranger Battalion to attack a known Viet Cong force located in a village less than five miles from Da Nang. Although successful—nine guerrillas were killed and four others were captured—it was not lost on anyone that the Viet Cong were now bold enough to operate within five miles of one of South Vietnam's major cities. In another demonstration of the Communists' strength and audacity, a large insurgent force attacked and overran an ARVN outpost only four-and-a-half miles from the provincial capital of Tam Ky two days later. Although a quick response by ARVN units supported by U.S. Marine and Army helicopters resulted in 70 Communists killed and 39 weapons captured, the attack on the outpost was not without cost. In total, 8 ARVN soldiers and 1 U.S. advisor had been killed; 20 ARVN soldiers and an Australian advisor had been wounded; and the insurgents had demonstrated that they could attack and decimate a well-fortified government outpost within miles of a provincial capital.

As the new year progressed, American forces continued to find themselves in the sights of Communist forces. On 7

February 1965, the Viet Cong attacked the American military compound at Pleiku in the Central Highlands with mortars, killing 9 Americans, wounding more than 100 others, and damaging or destroying 20 aircraft. On 10 February, 23 American soldiers were killed and 21 others were wounded in an attack on an enlisted barracks in the coastal city of Qui Nhon. In the space of slightly more than two months, Communist forces had demonstrated their ability to successfully execute major attacks on South Vietnamese and U.S. forces at widely separated locations throughout South Vietnam. In the face of these escalating attacks—particularly increasing direct attacks on U.S. personnel and facilities—the decision to increase U.S. troop strengths to protect American forces in ꞏSouth Vietnam could no longer be postponed.

Marine Forces Engaged

U.S. political leadership had been closely watching the unstable and rapidly deteriorating political and military situation in South Vietnam since the military-led coup against President Diem in November 1963. As 1964 drew to a close— "the end of a full decade of American political, economic, and military advice and assistance to South Vietnam," as the official Marine history phrased it—knowledgeable leaders in Washington and South Vietnam were coming to realize that the direct intervention of U.S. combat forces would be required to block the Communist takeover of South Vietnam and all of Indochina.

The possible employment of American forces in South Vietnam was of particular interest to the Marine Corps as nearly all of the combat-ready forces located in the Far East were Marines. The 3d MarDiv, with its headquarters and forces on the island of Okinawa, made up the bulk of these combat-ready ground forces. The 1st MAW, with its headquarters in Iwakuni, Japan, and its air groups located both in Japan and on Okinawa, made up the air support side of the Marine combat forces. These major units had been task organized in various operational contingency plans and could deploy in any size depending upon the mission assigned. The largest task organization, the III Marine Expeditionary Force (III MEF), would employ the entire division and aircraft wing, as well as their combat service support elements. At the other end of the spectrum, a Marine expeditionary unit would employ a battalion landing team, a composite aircraft squadron of fixed-wing aircraft and helicopters, and a small combat service support element. While these task organizations existed on paper, they could be assembled quickly to support the requirements of the U.S. political and military leadership.

Soon after the Gulf of Tonkin incident early in August 1964, the 9th MEB was activated by CinCPac. This transformed the 9th MEB from a paper organization into a combat force capable of landing on very short notice anywhere it was needed. It consisted of the 9th Marines regimental headquarters with three battalion landing teams and their attachments, a composite Marine air group with both fixed-wing aircraft and helicopters, and a combat support group. On 6 August 1964, about 6,000 of the 9th MEB's Marines—mostly the ground combat element—were embarked on Seventh Fleet amphibious shipping. The air elements—the fixed-wing aircraft were located at Iwakuni and the helicopters were on Okinawa—were alerted but not embarked. As the Gulf of Tonkin crisis abated, Admiral Ulysses S. Grant Sharp, USN, CinCPac, called for a relaxation of the alert status of the 9th MEB, and elements of the regimental landing team disembarked from their ships. One battalion landing team returned to Okinawa, a second was sent to the Philippines, and the third remained aboard Seventh Fleet ships as a part of the Special Landing Force. The expeditionary brigade's respite did not last long.

After the Communists' 1 November attack on the Bien Hoa air base, President Johnson ordered a month-long review of U.S. policy regarding North Vietnam. The review resulted in an early December plan to expand the air war in an attempt to discourage the North Vietnamese from supporting Communist efforts in the south. Air strikes against North Vietnamese infiltration routes would be increased, and a "continuous program of progressively more serious air strikes" against North Vietnam would be initiated if the North did not moderate its behavior. The Communists' response included the Christmas Eve bombing of the U.S. officers' quarters in Saigon and the infiltration of the 32d and 101st North Vietnamese Army regiments—uncovered by USMACV intelligence agents—into South Vietnam. If the Viet Cong and their North Vietnamese supporters were intimidated by the threat of increased U.S. air strikes, they were doing little to show it.

President Johnson responded quickly to the 7 February 1965 attacks at Pleiku, ordering reprisal air attacks—code named Flaming Dart—against targets in North Vietnam. Washington also authorized air strikes against Communist forces in the south. On 19 February, the first U.S. air strike—a bombing mission executed by Air Force B-57 aircraft—was flown in support of South Vietnamese ground troops. Five days later, the Air Force flew a second major mission in the Central Highlands in support of ARVN troops that had been ambushed by Communist forces. Further, to protect the growing number of U.S. military personnel and equipment at Da Nang, the president announced on 7 February that he was ordering the deployment of a Marine light antiaircraft missile battalion to Da Nang. Moreover, in a sign of the disintegrating situation in South Vietnam, he also directed the orderly "withdrawal of 1,800 dependents of American military men and civilians in South Viet-Nam."

The 1st Light Antiaircraft Missile Battalion, which had arrived on Okinawa in November from Marine Corps Base, Twentynine Palms, California, wasted no time deploying to South Vietnam. On the evening of 7 February, Lieutenant Colonel Bertram E. Cook Jr., the battalion commander, ordered Battery A, commanded by Captain Leon E. Obenhaus, to deploy to Da Nang. At 1045 on 8 February, the first Air Force transport aircraft carrying elements of Battery A left the runway at Okinawa. By close of business on 9 February, 52 Air Force transports had delivered 309 passengers and 315 tons of the battalion's equipment to Da Nang. Battery A, which set up on the northwest side of Da Nang's runway, was prepared to fire less than 12 hours after the first transport aircraft had touched down. By 16 February, the remainder of the battalion—less Battery C, which remained on Okinawa—had arrived at Da Nang aboard the attack cargo ship USS *Washburn* (AKA 108) and dock landing ship USS *Gunston Hall* (LSD 5). Two days later the tank landing ship, USS *Vernon County*, arrived from Okinawa with Company C, 7th Engineer Battalion, whose mission was to provide construction support for the light antiaircraft missile battalion. With the arrival of the engineers, the light antiaircraft missile battalion's deployment was complete.

While senior U.S. government policy makers were making decisions to increase support for South Vietnam and the Marines were actually deploying there, the government

of South Vietnam was continuing in a downward spiral. By mid-February, General Khanh, who had weathered several coup attempts during his year in power, was again in a fight for his political life. This time, he did not prevail. On 21 February, Khanh was deposed by a group of general officers led by General Nguyen Van Thieu, the IV Corps commander, and Air Vice Marshall Nguyen Cao Ky, commander of the VNAF. The United States now had a new South Vietnamese leadership to deal with.

During this period of increasing Communist military activity and South Vietnamese political and military disintegration, U.S. political and military officials continued to assess the situation. Reporting after the 7 February Communist attack on Pleiku, presidential special assistant McGeorge Bundy noted that the situation was "deteriorating, and without new U.S. action, defeat appears inevitable—probably not in a matter of weeks or perhaps even months, but within a year or so. There is still time to turn it around, but not much." General Westmoreland believed that it would take a U.S. division to protect American personnel and equipment in Vietnam from increasing Viet Cong attacks. On 11 February, the JCS provided the secretary of defense with a list of "reprisal options" to be taken against the Communists. While the JCS noted that "retaliatory air raids against North Vietnam had not achieved the intended effect," they recommended more of the same. They also suggested naval bombardment, covert operations, intelligence patrols, cross-border operations into Laos, and landing U.S. troops in South Vietnam.

In response, on 2 March 1965, President Johnson—postponing the almost-certain commitment of U.S. ground combat forces—authorized a "limited and measured" air campaign against North Vietnam. Code-named Rolling Thunder, it represented a marked departure from the reprisal raids that characterized Operation Flaming Dart. With Operation Rolling Thunder, the United States had transitioned "from the earlier reprisal type raids to a continuing air campaign based upon strategic considerations."

Earlier, on 22 February 1965, General Westmoreland requested the deployment of the 9th MEB to South Vietnam to adequately secure American forces, aircraft, and equipment at Da Nang. Admiral Sharp signaled to the JCS that he was in agreement with Westmoreland, and by the end of February, President Johnson had decided to commit the expeditionary brigade with two battalion landing teams to the defense of the airfield at Da Nang. After Ambassador Maxwell Taylor secured agreements with the South Vietnamese government and a recommendation to deploy a less-conspicuous U.S. Army airborne brigade by air from Okinawa (so as not to alarm the South Vietnamese people) was overruled, the JCS issued the order to immediately land the 9th MEB with its landing teams on 7 March 1965 (6 March in Washington).

Prior to this, Brigadier General Frederick J. Karch, the 3d MarDiv assistant division commander, had assumed command of the 9th MEB on 22 January 1965. A veteran of several World War II amphibious operations, his next two-and-a-half months would be characterized by hectic schedules as political instability and Buddhist-fomented antigovernment activities in South Vietnam, as well as decisions by U.S. political and military leaders, inexorably drew his command closer to becoming the first major U.S. ground combat unit to deploy to South Vietnam. BLTs 1/9 and 3/9—ground combat elements of the 9th MEB—had been deployed on board the Seventh Fleet's Naval Task Force 76 amphibious ships since the beginning of the year. On 23 January, Admiral Sharp relaxed 9th MEB's alert status. BLT 1/9, embarked on Naval Task Group 76.5 ships, assumed a 96-hour reaction time for deployment to South Vietnam as the task group assumed a position 70 miles southeast of Saigon. BLT 3/9 resumed its normal operations.

The 9th MEB waited, but it did not have to wait long. Buddhist-led antigovernment riots in Saigon and the former imperial capital of Hue on 22 and 23 January 1965 precipitated a change in South Vietnam's government. That brought BLT 1/9 and its amphibious ships, which had been steaming to Hong Kong for liberty, back to their position southeast of Saigon. BLT 3/9, embarked on Naval Task Group 76.7 ships, arrived off the coast of Da Nang on 29 January. With the formation of an interim government, the Marines' alert status was once again relaxed. With the commitment of the 9th MEB once again uncertain, General Karch spent 26–30 January at a Subic Bay planning conference for a Marine expeditionary brigade-size exercise scheduled for March in Thailand.

With the political and military situations continuing to deteriorate, General Westmoreland requested on 22 February that two of the 9th MEB's battalion landing teams be landed and that the third remain afloat off the South Vietnamese coast. BLT 1/9 and BLT 2/9, both back on board amphibious shipping, were close at hand off of the South Vietnamese coast. General Karch and the Navy task force commander, Rear Admiral Don W. Wulzen, were on board the Task Force 76 flagship, the USS *Mount McKinley* (AGC 7), also steaming off the coast of Vietnam. The command and ground elements were in position.

Coordination, briefings, and planning continued. On 25 February, General Karch and members of his staff met with General Westmoreland for discussions of the proposed Da Nang landing. Karch then flew to Da Nang to effect coordination of his plans with the South Vietnamese I Corps commander, Major General Nguyen Chanh Thi. With that accomplished, the general and his staff departed for Okinawa. Once there, they drafted 9th MEB Operational Plan 37D-65, which provided for the amphibious landing of one battalion landing team and the airlift of a second from Okinawa to Da Nang. To assess the viability of this plan, the MEB staff conducted a command post exercise on Okinawa.

At the beginning of March 1965, General Karch and his staff were still on Okinawa. Decisions were being finalized at the highest U.S. political and military levels, but the general's 9th MEB had still not received its deployment order. To prepare his Okinawa-based battalion—1st Battalion, 3d Marines—General Karch scheduled a two-day map exercise of the Da Nang area and a briefing for Lieutenant Colonel Herbert J. Bain, the commanding officer. Both activities were cancelled when, on 2 March, Karch received orders to proceed directly to Da Nang. At 2300 that same day, the general and 28 members of his staff departed Okinawa in a Marine KC-130. With a short stop at Cubi Point in the Philippines to take staff members of Navy Task Force 76 on board, the KC-130 continued its journey, landing in Da Nang on the morning of 3 March. General Karch and the Marine Corps–Navy group were met by USMACV liaison officers who provided a tour of the Da Nang air base and the landing beaches. At day's end, Karch and his staff were back on board their aircraft and headed for Subic Bay in the Philippines.

With decisions made and agreements secured with the government of South Vietnam, General Karch, issued a warning order to BLT 3/9 on 4 March to be prepared to "administratively land the landing force." Lieutenant Colonel

Marines from BLT 3/9 come ashore on 8 March 1965 at Red Beach 2, northwest of Da Nang. The heavy surf delayed the landing for an hour, with the fourth and final assault wave arriving ashore at 0918.

Defense Department (Marine Corps) A183676

Charles E. McPartlin Jr. and his battalion had been on ships steaming off the coast of South Vietnam since early February. Upon returning to the *Mount McKinley*, some 10 miles off the coast of Da Nang, General Karch assured Colonel McPartlin that he would control all movement on Red Beach 2—the designated landing area—and that the Vietnamese would regulate traffic along Route 1 from the beachhead, which was west of Da Nang and north of the airfield, to their positions at the airfield.

By 0545 on 8 March, the four ships of Amphibious Task Force 76 had closed on Da Nang harbor and anchored within 4,000 yards of the shore of Red Beach 2. At 0600, Admiral Wulzen, the task force commander, issued the order to "land the landing force." The weather and sea state—initially adequate with an intermittent drizzle, eight knot winds, and waves near the shoreline gentle and cresting at only two to four feet—rapidly deteriorated. By 0730, swells reaching 8 to 10 feet made the loading of small landing craft impossible. In light of this development, Admiral Wulzen delayed H-hour until 0900. At 0830, he reconfirmed the 0900 H-hour. The first wave of Marine assault troops in 11 amphibian tractors landed just three minutes after H-hour. By 0918, the fourth and final assault wave of BLT 3/9's Marines had come ashore. The Marines had landed, becoming the first major U.S. combat ground forces to be committed to the war in South Vietnam.

With his headquarters at Da Nang, General Karch soon had nearly 5,000 Marines under his command. They included Colonel McPartlin's BLT 3/9 that had landed amphibiously, Colonel Bain's BLT 1/3 that had flown in from Okinawa, two helicopter squadrons, and a limited brigade logistics support group. On 9 March, Task Unit 79.3.5, Marine Unit Vietnam (Shufly) was dissolved, redesignated Marine Air Group 16 (MAG-16), and made a subordinate element of the 9th MEB. Colonel John H. King Jr., formerly the Shufly commander, assumed command of the air group. HMM-163, the air group's helicopter squadron commanded by Lieutenant Colonel Norman G. Ewers, continued to fly most of its missions in support of the South Vietnamese. HMM-162, newly arrived and under the command of Colonel Curtis, became operational on 12 March and initially flew only in support of the 9th MEB. By month's end, both squadrons were flying support missions for both ARVN and Marine units.

In the early weeks of 1965, Lieutenant General Victor H. Krulak, then commander of FMFPac, had recognized that the deteriorating political and military situations in South Vietnam would soon require additional U.S. forces. In recognition of this requirement, General Krulak developed plans for the movement of major Marine Corps operational units from the West Coast and Hawaii to the Far East. In March, he executed those plans, and Marine air and ground combat units began flowing to the region, including two fixed-wing squadrons. Marine Attack Squadron 311 (VMA-311) departed the continental United States on 25 March and was closely followed two days later by Marine Fighter Attack Squadron 542 (VMFA-542). Upon their arrival in the Far East, both joined the 1st MAW.

General Krulak's plans also called for the deployment to the Far East of the Hawaii-based 1st Marine Brigade. Its 4th Marine Regiment, accompanied by the 3d Battalion, 12th Marine Artillery Regiment (a reconnaissance company and an antitank company), joined the 3d MarDiv on Okinawa at the end of March. Marine Aircraft Group 13 (MAG-13), the brigade's air group, became a part of Japan-based 1st MAW upon its arrival in the region, also at the end of March. Thus, General Krulak had successfully deployed his Marine combat forces forward. They were positioned and prepared to respond to any contingency.

That same month, General Westmoreland and the USMACV staff initiated a detailed assessment of the total U.S. effort in Vietnam "before making what may prove to be in the light of history, a momentous recommendation." On 26 March, with his assessment completed, Westmoreland recommended that the United States commit the equivalent of two divisions, with combat and service support, to the fight in South Vietnam. For the Marines, he recommended reinforcing the 9th MEB with two battalions: one assigned to the defense of U.S. personnel (specifically at a U.S. Army communications facility) and the Hue/Phu Bai air strip located about eight miles south of the old imperial capital of Hue, and the other assigned to Da Nang.

At a 1 April meeting, President Johnson approved General Westmoreland's recommendations. Further, the president substantially expanded the latitude under which Marines could operate in South Vietnam from a purely defensive posture to "active combat under conditions to be established and approved by the Secretary of Defense in consultation with the Secretary of State."

On 14 March 1965, the 3d MEB was activated by Major General William R. "Rip" Collins, commanding general of 3d MarDiv, to control the movement to South Vietnam of the 9th MEB's third and fourth battalions. On 4 April, Brigadier General Marion E. Carl, a World War II ace who had downed 18 Japanese aircraft, assumed command of the 3d MEB. The following day, he flew with his staff to Subic Bay where Admiral Wulzen and his staff stood ready to draft plans to support the deployments. As the *Mount McKinley*, bound for South Vietnam, steamed into the South China Sea, Admiral Wulzen's Task Force 76 and General Carl's 3d MEB staffs busied themselves drafting embarkation and landing plans. On 10 April, BLT 2/3 conducted an uneventful amphibious landing at Da Nang. A provisional task force of two rifle companies under the command of Colonel Clement was helilifted to Phu Bai to provide security until the arrival of BLT 3/4.

The movement of BLT 3/4 to the airfield at Phu Bai required a little more attention. Admiral Wulzen had expressed concern for the proposed transit of some elements of BLT 3/4 from amphibious ships in the South China Sea down the Song Huong (also known as the Hue or Perfume River) to landing sites at Hue. To assess the viability of the concept, General Carl, with four outboard motor boats provided to him by the Vietnamese, conducted a personal reconnaissance of the river. Over an approximately four-hour period, the general's small armada traveled from Hue up the Song Huong to the South China Sea and back. He determined the route to be both trafficable and safe and, in the process, convinced Admiral Wulzen and his staff. Over the period from 14 to 19 April, BLT 3/4 conducted its landing in South Vietnam. Before 0900 on 14 April, two companies had been landed across Red Beach 2 in Da Nang, from which they were flown to Phu Bai. Early on 15 April, employing LCMs (landing crafts, mechanized) and LCVPs (landing crafts, vehicle, personnel), the remaining Marines of BLT 3/4 departed their amphibious ships for the 11-mile journey to the landing sites at Hue. From there, they were transported to Phu Bai by trucks. When the operation was completed on 19 April, U.S. Navy landing craft had made 263 trips to the Hue landing sites, carrying 1,371 tons of cargo and traveling 6,000

miles. With its mission completed, General Carl's 3d MEB staff returned to Okinawa where the unit was (temporarily) deactivated.

Additional aviation units were added to the 9th MEB's T/O before the end of April. On 16 April, Marine Air Support Squadron 2 (MASS-2) debarked amphibious ships in Da Nang harbor and proceeded to the airfield. Commanded by Lieutenant Colonel Paul L. Hitchcock, MASS-2 provided a direct air support center and an air support radar team for deployed Marine aviation units. On 17 April, Lieutenant Colonel Otis W. Corman, commanding the Marine Composite Reconnaissance Squadron One (VMCJ-1), flew into the Da Nang air base with six Douglas EF-10B Skynights (formerly designated F3D-2Q). This squadron provided all the Services with electronic countermeasures support.

As April drew to a close, General Karch's 9th MEB numbered 8,878 Marines and sailors. It included a regiment with four battalions, a four-squadron air group, artillery and engineer units, and a logistics support group. During April, its operational charter was once again expanded. On 14 April, General Westmoreland provided the Marine expeditionary brigade with a concept of operations that directed it to "undertake in coordination with RVN I Corps, an intensifying program of offensive operations to fix and destroy the Viet Cong in the general Da Nang area."

Additional Combat Forces Committed

U.S. civilian and military planners at the highest levels remained preoccupied with assessments of the gravity of the situation in South Vietnam and the number of U.S. troops that would be required to effect a favorable outcome. In search of a solution, Secretary of Defense McNamara; Assistant Secretary of Defense for International Security Affairs John McNaughton; Ambassador to South Vietnam Maxwell Taylor; Chairman of the Joint Chiefs of Staff General Earle G. Wheeler, USA; General Westmoreland; and Admiral Sharp held a conference at CinCPac headquarters in Honolulu, Hawaii, on 20 April 1965. Their consensus was that their Communist adversaries were capable of and were planning significantly increased offensive operations in South Vietnam and that additional U.S. forces would be required to successfully combat them. Accordingly, they recommended that an additional 42,000 U.S. military personnel be deployed to

Vietnam. For the Marines, the conferees recommended that a force composed of three reinforced infantry battalions and three jet aircraft squadrons—approximately 5,000 Marines—be deployed to Chu Lai, a provincial capital 57 miles southeast of Da Nang. There, the Marines would construct an airfield and establish a third enclave (the first two being Da Nang and Hue/Phu Bai). On 30 April, President Johnson approved the Honolulu Conference recommendations.

The designation of Chu Lai as the site for the Marines' next enclave resulted from a months-long debate in the Pentagon over a suitable site for an expeditionary airfield south of Da Nang. General Krulak had visited the area in 1964 and determined it to be a good site for the construction of a short airfield for tactical support (SATS). The SATS airfield, constructed with prefabricated metal runways and taxi strips, was a Marine Corps concept still in its early stages. Secretary McNamara had tentatively approved construction of the airfield in late March, but final approval did not come until the Honolulu Conference ended in late April. In a presentation to the conference attendees, the U.S. Pacific Air Forces command stated that construction of a concrete airfield at Chu Lai would take approximately 11 months. When asked by the secretary of defense "how long" it would take the Marines to establish a SATS site adequate to support the proposed mission, General Krulak told the secretary that the Marines could do it in 25 days.

On 28 April, the 3d MEB was reactivated as the command element for the Chu Lai operation. The 3d MEB's ground combat element included Regimental Landing Team 4 (RLT 4), commanded by Colonel Edward P. Dupras Jr. RLT 4 included BLT 1/4, commanded by Lieutenant Colonel Harold D. Fredericks; BLT 2/4, commanded by Lieutenant Colonel Joseph R. Fischer; and 3d Reconnaissance Battalion, commanded by Lieutenant Colonel Don H. Blanchard. On General Westmoreland's recommendation, a third Marine infantry battalion—BLT 3/3—was added to the 3d MEB T/O on 2 May. It came ashore after the initial landings. MABS-12, commanded by Lieutenant Colonel Alexander Wilson, was scheduled to come ashore during the initial assault. The plan called for the remainder of Marine Aircraft Group 12 (MAG-12) to deploy to Chu Lai when construction of the SATS airfield was completed. Naval Mobile Construction Battalion 10 was attached to the 3d MEB for

construction of the airfield. On 29 April, General Carl and his staff flew to the Philippines for planning sessions with Admiral Wulzen and his staff on board the amphibious flag ship USS Estes (ACG 12).

H-hour was set for 0800 on 7 May 1965. With the ships of the amphibious task force in the area, BLT 2/4 and Companies C and D of BLT 1/4 began their ship-to-shore movement. To ensure that the landing would be unopposed as assumed during planning, combat units from the ARVN's 2d Division had secured the Chu Lai environs with Company K, BLT 3/9, providing additional beach security. After landing, two companies from BLT 1/4 moved inland approximately three miles to secure Landing Zone Robin, which overlooked Route 1. With that accomplished, Lieutenant Colonel Gene W. Morrison's Marine Medium Helicopter Squadron 161 (HMM-161) flew in BLT 1/4's remaining two companies. By day's end, Colonel Dupras had moved his RLT 4 headquarters ashore and established a defensive perimeter from Ky Ha Peninsula in the north to high ground in the west and to the South China Sea three miles south of Red Beach. The 3d Reconnaissance Battalion screened the 3d MEB's southern flank until relieved by elements of BLT 3/3, which began coming ashore when they arrived from Okinawa on 12 May. By then, when the amphibious operation was officially terminated, more than 10,925 tons of equipment and supplies had been off-loaded and moved across the beach.

With the conclusion of the amphibious operations at Chu Lai, the 3d MarDiv had seven of its nine infantry battalions and nearly all of its artillery regiment in South Vietnam. Further, the Marine Corps had also committed a major portion of its Far East–based 1st MAW. Two separate Marine expeditionary brigade–size combat organizations—each commanded by a brigadier general—were deployed and conducting combat operations in South Vietnam with no coordinating and supporting senior headquarters. In anticipation of this situation, on 5 May 1965, the JCS had signaled the president's approval for the establishment in Da Nang of a "force/division/wing headquarters to include the CG [commanding general], 3d Marine Division, and 1st Marine Aircraft Wing." The following day, General Collins established the headquarters of III MEF and the 3d MarDiv in Da Nang and assumed command of both. The 9th MEB was deactivated, and General Karch returned to Okinawa to take charge of the remaining 3d MarDiv units there. Subsequent to the completion of 3d MEB's landing at Chu Lai, General Carl assumed duties as the deputy commander of the III Marine Amphibious Force (III MAF), as the senior Marine headquarters had been designated on 7 May. Changing the name of the III MEF to III MAF was a bow to the sensitivities of the South Vietnamese. General Westmoreland believed the term "expeditionary" would have unpleasant connotations for the Vietnamese. And, although a III Marine Amphibious Corps had existed in the Pacific during World War II, Marine advisors to the CMC thought that the term "Corps" might also offend them. General Greene therefore decided on the term "Marine Amphibious Force" for Marine forces in Vietnam.

Additional Marine combat, combat support, and combat service support units then flowed to South Vietnam, rapidly growing III MAF in the process. By the end of May, more than 17,000 Marines populated units in Vietnam. By the end of July, that number had doubled to 34,000. And by 31 December 1965, the number of Marines in South Vietnam topped 39,000. Many thousands more would arrive in the years ahead.

Epilogue

The United States had finally crossed the line. It had committed major U.S. ground combat units, including Marines, to the fight in South Vietnam. And although the 7 March landing order from the JCS clearly stated that "the U.S. Marine Force will not, repeat will not, engage in day-to-day actions against the Viet Cong," Communist successes and South Vietnamese ineptitude left no doubt that the Marines would soon assume an offensive posture.

The major U.S. policy makers and senior military officers recognized clearly that the South Vietnamese government and its military were not up to the task of defending their country against the Viet Cong and its allies from North Vietnam. Absent substantial military support from the United States, they would surely lose. As McGeorge Bundy had noted, it was only a matter of time.

The U.S. political leadership saw such an outcome as inimical to its national interest. It could not allow South Vietnam—and then, perhaps, all of Southeast Asia—to fall to the Communists.

The introduction of major U.S. combat forces into South Vietnam had a deleterious effect on the strategic timetable of the Viet Cong and their North Vietnamese masters. In 1964 and early 1965, they had enjoyed major successes against their less talented and less aggressive South Vietnamese adversaries. They had gone toe-to-toe with their enemies at the multiregiment and division levels and had won decisive victories on the battlefield. They had been moving steadily toward a general offensive, phase III of Mao Tse-tung's three-phase template on revolutionary warfare.

The arrival of the Americans upset their timetable throughout South Vietnam. In some places, the Communists had to fall back to (or remain in) Mao's phase II (mobile warfare) or even phase I (guerrilla operations). Mao's template provided for this and the Communists accepted it. They were patient men. They had been fighting for independence since the second decade of the twentieth century. They had defeated the French; now they faced the Americans. They would adjust and continue the struggle. They believed that time was on their side and that, in time, they would prevail. This was the enemy the U.S. Marines came to fight in the spring of 1965.

Sources

The material in this work was derived from the following sources: Capt Robert H. Whitlow, *U.S. Marines in Vietnam: The Advisory & Combat Assistance Era, 1954–1964,* Washington, DC: History and Museums Division, Headquarters, U.S. Marine Corps, 1977. Maj J. M. Yingling, Capt H. D. Bradshaw, and B. M. Frank, *United States Marine Corps Activities in Vietnam, 1954–1963: A Historical Monograph Prepared for the Secretary of Defense,* Washington, DC: Historical Branch, G-3 Division, Headquarters, Marine Corps, undated. (This document can be found in the Archives Section of the Gray Research Center at Quantico, VA.) MABS-16 (Rein) AAR, "Report of Operation Millpond, Udorn, Thailand, March–October 1961, MABS-16 (Rein) dated 2 November 1961." (This document can be found at the National Archives, RG 127, Box 85, #19.) 3d Marine Expeditionary Unit special report, 16 May–7 Aug 1962, forwarded by Commanding General, 3dMEU ltr 103/GPA/gtp, Ser: 0015662, dtd 1 Sep 1962, subj: Special Report of MCC 116/3dMEU Deployment to Thailand from 16 May 1962 to 7 August 1962. Jack Shulimson and Maj Charles M. Johnson, *U.S. Marines in Vietnam: The Landing and the Buildup, 1965,* Washington, DC: History and Museums Division, Headquarters, U.S. Marine Corps, 1978. Mark Atwood Lawrence and Frederik Logevall, introduction to *The First Vietnam War: Colonial Conflict and Cold War Crisis,* Lawrence and Logevall, eds. (Cambridge, MA: Harvard University Press, 2007).

John Prados, *The Blood Road—The Ho Chi Minh Trail and the Vietnam War,* New York: John Wiley & Sons, Inc., 1999. Mark Moyar, *Triumph Forsaken: The First Vietnam War,* New York: Cambridge University Press, 2006. Commanding General, FMFPac ltr 0007362, dtd 25Jan62 to CMC (Code AO3), Subj: Marine Corps participation in operations in Southeast Asia, 25 Jan 1962 (Gray Research Center, Quantico, VA). LtCol John J. Cahill and Jack Shulimson, *History of U.S. Marine Corps Operations in Vietnam, January–June 1965,* Washington, DC: Historical Branch, G-3 Division, Headquarters, U.S. Marine Corps, 1969. Maj T. C. Edwards, "3dMarDiv Counter Guerrilla Training," *Marine Corps Gazette,* May63. MajGen Gene A. Deegan, USMC (Ret.), intvw with author, 13Apr2008. Martin Stuart-Fox, *A History of Laos,* New York: Cambridge University Press, 1997. "Laos: Americans at Work,"

Time, 7Apr61. "Laos Drops Paratroop Force to Cut Off a Rebel Spearhead," *New York Times,* 6Apr61. Crosby S. Hoyes, "Marines in Thailand Tight-Lipped but Alert," *Evening Star,* 25Mar61. LtCol Archie J. Clapp, "Shu-Fly Diary," *U.S. Naval Institute Proceedings,* October 1963. "U.S. Marines to Fly Into Viet-Nam Today," *Washington Post,* 15Apr62. Homer Bigart, "Marine 'Copters Land In Vietnam," *New York Times,* 16Apr62. "U.S. Marines' 'Copter Task Unit Set to Act After Day in Vietnam," *New York Times,* 17Apr62. Tillman Durbin, "U.S. Role In Vietnam Holds Many Risks," *New York Times,* 22Apr62. Marine Corps Operational Analysis Group, Study No. 1, "Characteristics of U.S. Marine Helicopter Operations in the Mekong Delta,"12Mar63. Joe D'Arcangelo, author intvw, 11March09. Commanding Officer, HMM-163 ltr to Commanding Officer, MAG-16, Subj: Summary of HMM-163 Operations during period 16Sep62 to 11Jan 63, 15Feb63. Anonymous author, "Officers of '163 Pin Crew Wings on 44 Enlisteds," *Loose Wing Gossip,* the MAG-16, MCAF, Futema, Special Services Newsletter, 33-63, dtd 23Aug63. LtGen Ormond R. Simpson, USMC (Ret.), intvw with Dr. Terry Anderson and Benis M. Frank, 1985 (History and Museums Division, Headquarters, Washington, DC). BLT 3/9, Command Diary, Report Symbol MC-5750-02, 17May62–29Jul62. David H. Hugel, "SHUFLY Memories: A Personal Look At Marine Corps Aviation's Beachhead in Vietnam," *The Flightline—1st Marine Aircraft Association—Vietnam Service,* vol. 4, no. 2, Summer97. Commanding General, FMFPac, ltr 20IEO/mbh, over 0041664, dtd 25Jun64, to Distribution List, subj: "On-Job-Training, Republic of Vietnam; March 1964 report compilation." David H. Hugel, "Covering Early Marine Corps Operations in Vietnam," *Leatherneck,* Apr03. Anonymous author, "HMM-361 Marines Lauded," *Torii Teller,* MCAS, Iwakuni, Japan, vol. 9, no. 21, dtd 28Feb64. Rick Newman and Don Sheppard, *Bury Us Upside Down: The Misty Pilots and the Secret Battle for the Ho Chi Minh Trail,* New York: Ballantine Books, 2006. John G. Norris, "Retaliatory Strike Made After Major Red Attacks; Marine Force Is Shifted," *Washington Post,* 8Feb65. Graham Cosmas, *The Joint Chiefs of Staff and the War in Vietnam, 1960–1968,* Part 2 (Washington DC: Office of Joint History, Office of the Chairman of the Joint Chiefs of Staff, 2012). "Major Battles Rage Near Strategic Viet Air Base," *Los Angeles Times,* 10Feb65.

George R. Hofmann Jr.
Colonel, U.S. Marine Corps (Retired)

Photo courtesy of the author

George Hofmann joined the U.S. Marine Corps as a private in 1959 and retired as a colonel in 1992. Highlights of his career include two tours in Vietnam (he served as a platoon commander and the logistics officer with the 2d Battalion, 5th Marines, in Hue City during the 1968 Tet Offensive); command of the 1st Reconnaissance Battalion; and command of Camp Fuji, the Marine Corps' training facility on the island of Honshu, Japan. Subsequent to leaving the Marine Corps, Hofmann earned a master's degree in geography from the George Washington University (GWU). He remained at GWU for seven additional years as an adjunct faculty member for the Department of Geography and the Elliott School of International Affairs, where he taught a course on military geography at both the undergraduate (lecture) and graduate (seminar) levels. When not traveling or trout fishing, George Hofmann resides in Sarasota, Florida.

www.ingramcontent.com/pod-product-compliance
Lightning Source LLC
Chambersburg PA
CBHW050503110426
42742CB00018B/3354

9 781947 403017